Keep ... en
you a ... in
the lo...y.

Whether you are in your car or on foot, you will enjoy an evocative journey back in time. Compare the Ipswich of old with what you can see today—see how the streets of the town and its parks and open spaces have changed; examine the shops and buildings and notice how they have been altered or replaced; look at fine details such as lamp-posts, shop fascias and trade signs; and see the many alterations to Ipswich and its surrounding area that have taken place unnoticed during our lives, some of which we may have taken for granted.

At the turn of a page you will gain fascinating insights into the unique history of Ipswich.

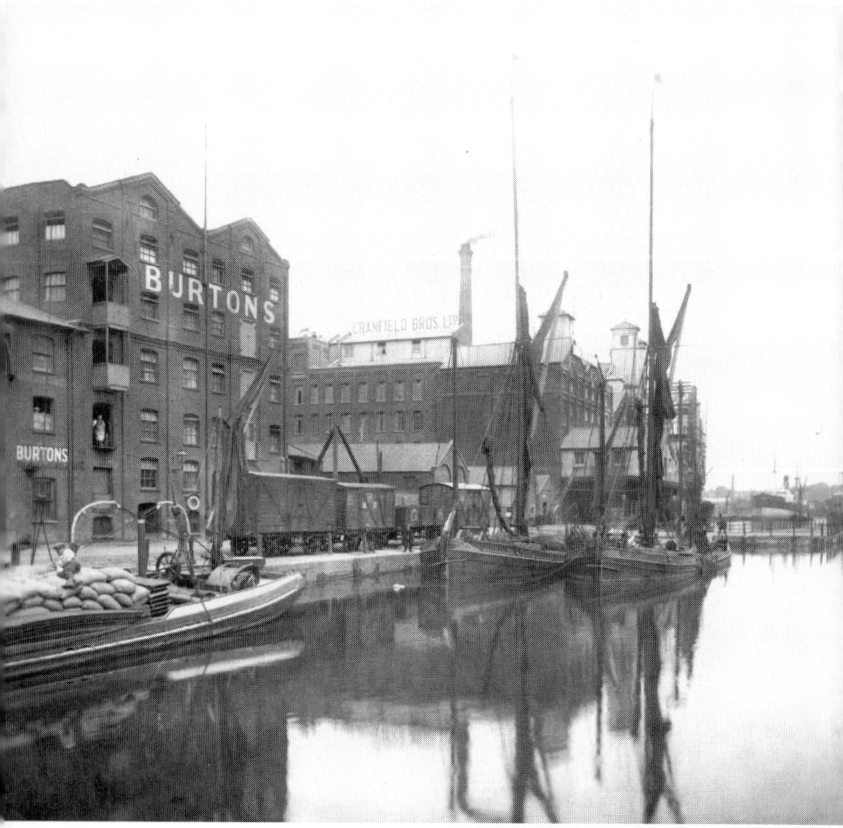

FRANCIS FRITH'S
pocket ALBUM

IPSWICH

A POCKET ALBUM

Adapted from an original book by
CLIVE TULLY

First published in the United Kingdom in 2005 by
Frith Book Company Ltd

ISBN 1-85937-949-4

British Library Cataloguing in Publication Data

Ipswich—A Pocket Album
Adapted from an original book by Clive Tully

Frith Book Company Ltd
Frith's Barn, Teffont,
Salisbury, Wiltshire SP3 5QP
Tel: +44 (0) 1722 716 376
Email: info@francisfrith.co.uk
www.francisfrith.co.uk

Printed and bound in Great Britain by MPG, Bodmin

Front Cover: **IPSWICH**, Corn Exchange 1893 32203T
The colour-tinting is for illustrative purposes only, and is not intended to be historically accurate.

Frontispiece: **IPSWICH**, St Peter's Dock 1921 70411

AS WITH ANY HISTORICAL DATABASE THE FRITH ARCHIVE IS CONSTANTLY BEING CORRECTED AND IMPROVED AND THE PUBLISHERS WOULD WELCOME INFORMATION ON OMISSIONS OR INACCURACIES

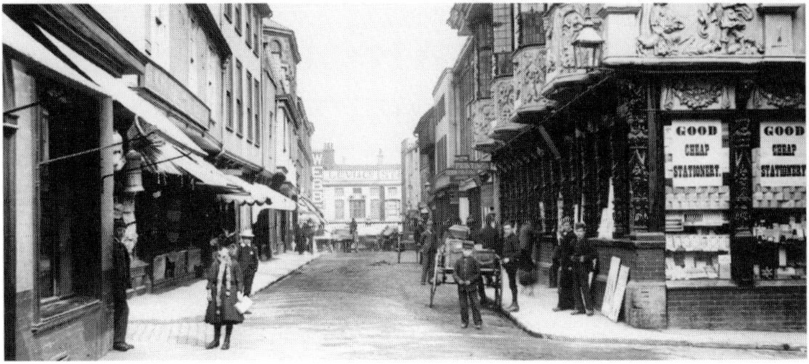

Butter Market 1893 / 32204

CONTENTS

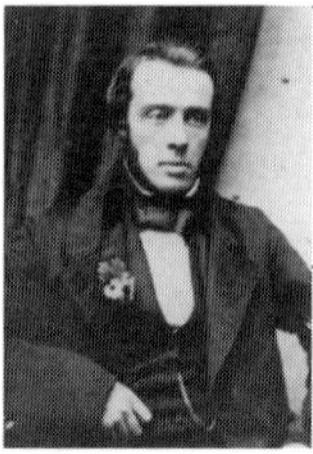

FRANCIS FRITH
VICTORIAN PIONEER

Francis Frith, founder of the world-famous photographic archive, was a complex and multi-talented man. A devout Quaker and a highly successful Victorian businessman, he was philosophic by nature and pioneering in outlook. By 1855 he had already established a wholesale grocery business in Liverpool, and sold it for the astonishing sum of £200,000, which is the equivalent today of over £15,000,000.Now in his thirties, and captivated by the new science of photography, Frith set out on a series of pioneering journeys up the Nile and to the Near East.

INTRIGUE AND EXPLORATION

He was the first photographer to venture beyond the sixth cataract of the Nile. Africa was still the mysterious 'Dark Continent', and Stanley and Livingstone's historic meeting was a decade into the future. The conditions for picture taking confound belief. He laboured for hours in his wicker dark-room in the sweltering heat of the desert, while the volatile chemicals fizzed dangerously in their trays. Back in London he exhibited his photographs and was 'rapturously cheered' by members of the Royal Society. His reputation as a photographer was made overnight.

VENTURE OF A LIFE-TIME

By the 1870s the railways had threaded their way across the country, and Bank Holidays and half-day Saturdays had been made obligatory by Act of Parliament. All of a sudden the working man and his family were able to enjoy days out, take holidays, and see a little more of the world.

With typical business acumen, Francis Frith foresaw that these new tourists would enjoy having souvenirs to commemorate their days out. For the next thirty years he travelled the country by train and by pony and trap, producing fine photographs of seaside resorts and beauty spots that were keenly bought by millions of Victorians. These prints were painstakingly pasted into family albums and pored over during the dark nights of winter, rekindling precious memories of summer excursions. Frith's studio was soon supplying retail shops all over the country, and by 1890 F Frith & Co had become the greatest specialist photographic publishing company in the world, with over 2,000 sales outlets, and pioneered the picture postcard.

FRANCIS FRITH'S LEGACY

Francis Frith had died in 1898 at his villa in Cannes, his great project still growing. The archive he created continued in business for another seventy years. By 1970 it contained over a third of a million pictures showing 7,000 British towns and villages.

Frith's legacy to us today is of immense significance and value, for the magnificent archive of evocative photographs he created provides a unique record of change in the cities, towns and villages throughout Britain over a century and more. Frith and his fellow studio photographers revisited locations many times down the years to update their views, compiling for us an enthralling and colourful pageant of British life and character.

We are fortunate that Frith was dedicated to recording the minutiae of everyday life. For it is this sheer wealth of visual data, the painstaking chronicle of changes in dress, transport, street layouts, buildings, housing, engineering and landscape that captivates us so much today, offering us a powerful link with the past and with the lives of our ancestors.

Computers have now made it possible for Frith's many thousands of images to be accessed almost instantly. The archive offers every one of us an opportunity to examine the places where we and our families have lived and worked down the years. Its images, depicting our shared past, are now bringing pleasure and enlightenment to millions around the world a century and more after his death.

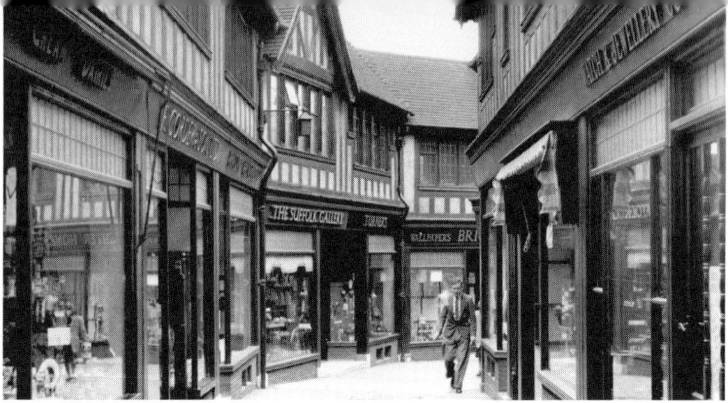

THE WALK C1955 I18030

IPSWICH
AN INTRODUCTION

MANY people tend to draw a comparison between Ipswich and Norwich as the major towns in their respective counties. If nothing else, an East Anglian derby match between Norwich City and Ipswich Town football clubs excites far more local passion than if either team were playing Manchester United! Although both towns are founded on ancient communities, Ipswich is more important than Norwich as a port - and indeed, it always has been. It is situated at the point where the freshwater River Gipping joins the head of the tidal Orwell Estuary, and even as far back as the 7th century Ipswich was not merely a trading port, it was the biggest in the country. Known then as Gippeswic, this Anglo-Saxon port survived many Viking raids. It very quickly established itself as a place of industry, producing a distinctive grey type of pottery which we know was widely distributed, both throughout East Anglia and beyond. It is very likely that the close proximity of the East Anglian royal palace at Rendlesham had a marked bearing on the fortunes of the town, as much trade in imported fine wines, furs and textiles passed through here, as well as the products of the local industry being sent from here to other ports along the coast.

By the time of the Conquest, Ipswich had its own mint, and by the beginning of the 13th century the town's status was confirmed with its first charter, awarded by King John. The middle ages saw the town prosper through the East Anglian wool trade, and by the 17th century, there was also a thriving ship-building industry using Suffolk oak, with shipyards lining the banks of the Orwell. Indeed, in 1614, Ipswich was quoted as having more shipwrights than any port in England. In Georgian times, the town suffered a commercial decline, but its prosperity was restored by the Industrial Revolution, evidenced by the large number of 19th century houses in the town. Engineering businesses like Ransomes established themselves, producing everything from railway equipment to agricultural machinery.

But at the end of the 18th century, the most pressing problem was with the docks, where large ships were unable to berth. The river was silting up, and even at high tide it was becoming impossible to get upstream. The solution, which took another forty years, was to construct the Wet Dock by isolating a bend in the river and diverting the river itself into a bypass channel known as the New Cut. With lock gates to control access to it, the Wet Dock provided the means for ships to be able to dock at any state of the tide - at the time, it was the largest such enclosed area of water in Europe. Further improvements were made to the dock, but by the end of the First World War, the port had expanded beyond the Wet Dock - the river had been dredged and quays built to accommodate large ships. Ships do still unload in the Wet Dock, but increasingly it is being taken over by yachts and pleasure boats, while the cargo vessels unload at the riverside quays - the oil and grain terminals on the east bank, and the container and roll-on roll-off berths on the west.

The railway arrived in Ipswich in 1846, and with that came further expansion and improvements to the town's prosperity. However, it was not until 1860 that a tunnel was cut through Stoke Hill, thus enabling the line to be continued to Bury St Edmunds and Norwich.

The basic street pattern of the town centre is still that of the medieval town, including a fine range of buildings dating from the 15th century onwards. Like Norwich, Ipswich was once surrounded by a wall, a legacy of which can be found in many of the street names, such as Westgate and Northgate. Cornhill, with its flamboyant mock Italian and Jacobean-style buildings, is on the original site of the market place of the town; it was also the place where several 'heretics' were burned at the stake. One block away is the Buttermarket, which contains the town's most famous building, the Ancient House. Also known as Sparrowe's House, this remarkable building is over five hundred years old; the walls of its upper floors, with their bay windows, overhang the lower part. Its interest lies in the elaborate moulded plasterwork designs on its outer walls - it is probably the best surviving example of pargetting in Britain. The panels below the first floor windows represent the continents of the known world at that time - Europe, Asia, Africa and America - along with the arms of Charles II (who, it is said, hid here after the Battle of Worcester) over the main doorway.

Just to the west is the Unitarian Meeting House, built about 1700. Inside, four great wooden pillars, said to be from ships' masts, form part of the structure, while the carved pulpit is quite probably the work of Grinling Gibbons. It is likely that this building was one of the first purpose-built non-conformist chapels, the Toleration Act having been passed only ten years previously. On the corner where St Nicholas Street is joined by Silent Street stands a magnificent group of Tudor houses with a carved corner post. Cardinal Wolsey is reputed to have been born in this area, and a plaque on one of the houses commemorates this. Nearby is Wolsey's Gate, the only surviving part of Cardinal Wolsey's ambitious plan to build a College of Cardinals. The building was started in 1527, and would have been quite extensive. But

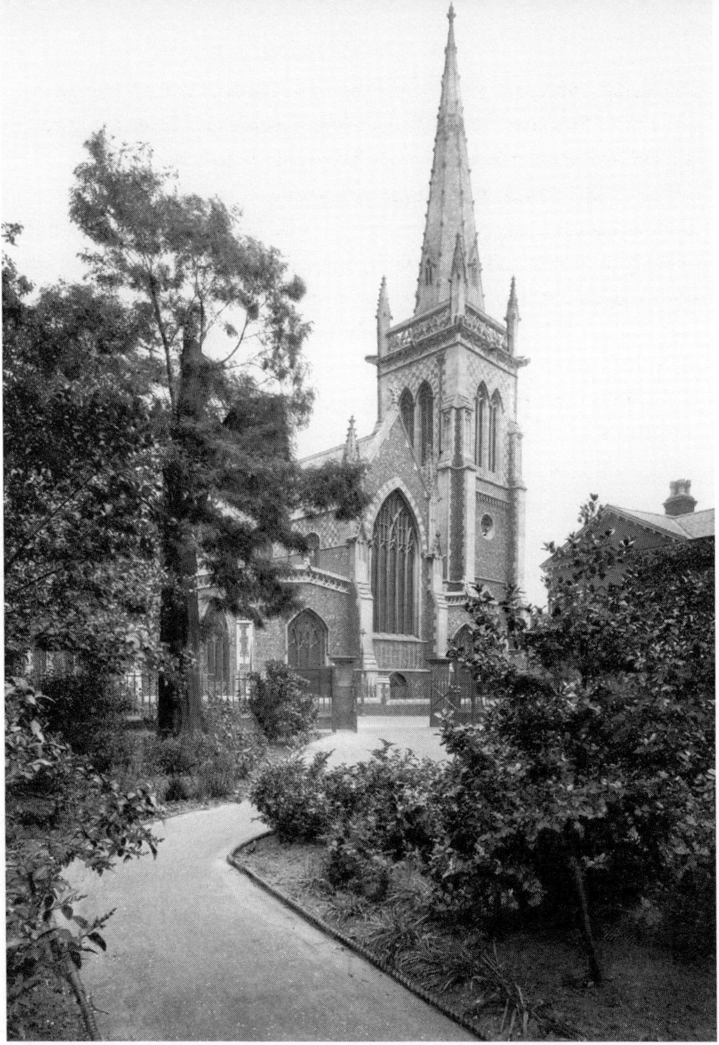

ST MARY LE TOWER

1921 / 70402

Wolsey fell from grace when he failed to support Henry VIII's wish to marry Anne Boleyn, and it was never completed. The brick gateway, with its barely discernible royal cipher, is all that remains.

Just a few years later, Christchurch Mansion was built on the site of the 12th century priory of the Holy Trinity. This Tudor country house is now a museum, and its adjoining art gallery houses a fine collection of paintings by Constable and Gainsborough. It is interesting to recall that this marvellous house almost became a housing estate in the late 19th century. The Cobbold brewing family bought the building and then presented it to the town, thus enabling us still to enjoy this monument to gracious living.

Tavern Street contains the Great White Horse Hotel, which, despite its Georgian facade, is a timber-framed building dating back to the 16th century. Famous visitors have included Dickens (who wrote about it in 'Pickwick Papers'), George II in 1736, Louis XVIII of France in 1807, and Lord Nelson in 1800. Opposite the hotel stands a group of buildings which appear to be Tudor, but are in fact reproductions, built in the 1930s when such imitations were in vogue. Today, despite the presence of the two major ports of Harwich and Felixstowe only ten miles away at the mouth of the Orwell, Ipswich remains an important industrial and commercial centre.

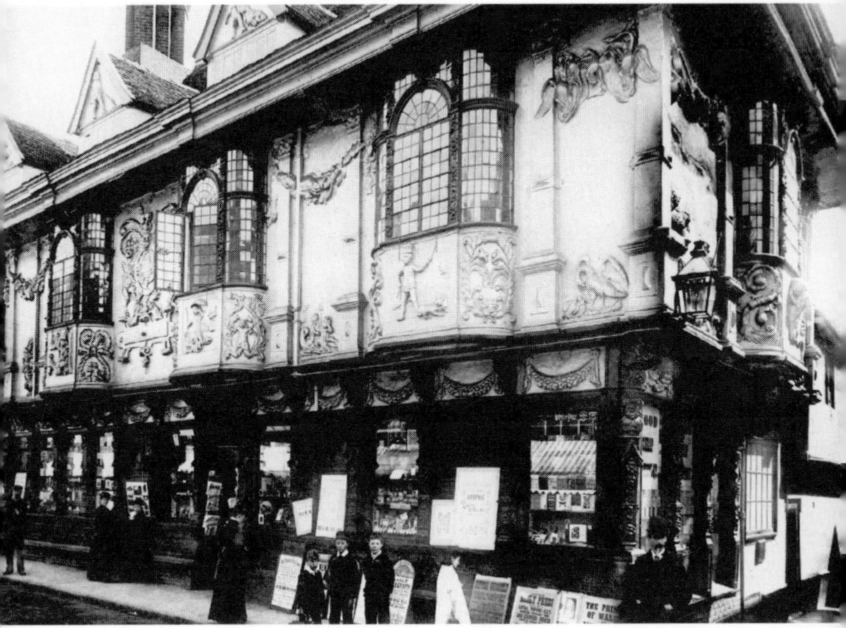

When this photograph was taken, the richly pargetted Ancient House, which dates back to medieval times, was occupied by Fred Pawsey, selling books and stationery.

THE ANCIENT HOUSE

1893 / 32205

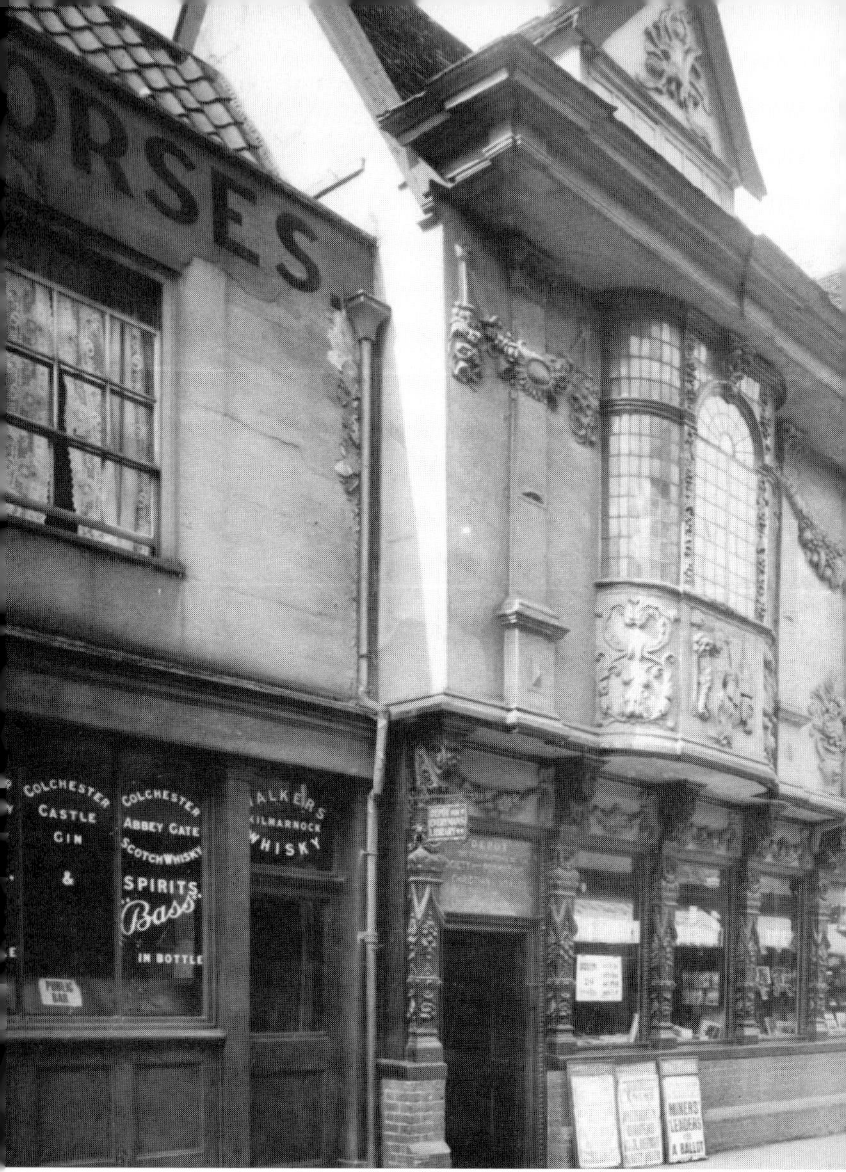
COLCHESTER
CASTLE
GIN
COLCHESTER
ABBEY GATE
SCOTCH WHISKY
&
SPIRITS
Bass
IN BOTTLE
ALKER'S
KILMARNOCK
WHISKY

THE ANCIENT HOUSE

1921 / 70399

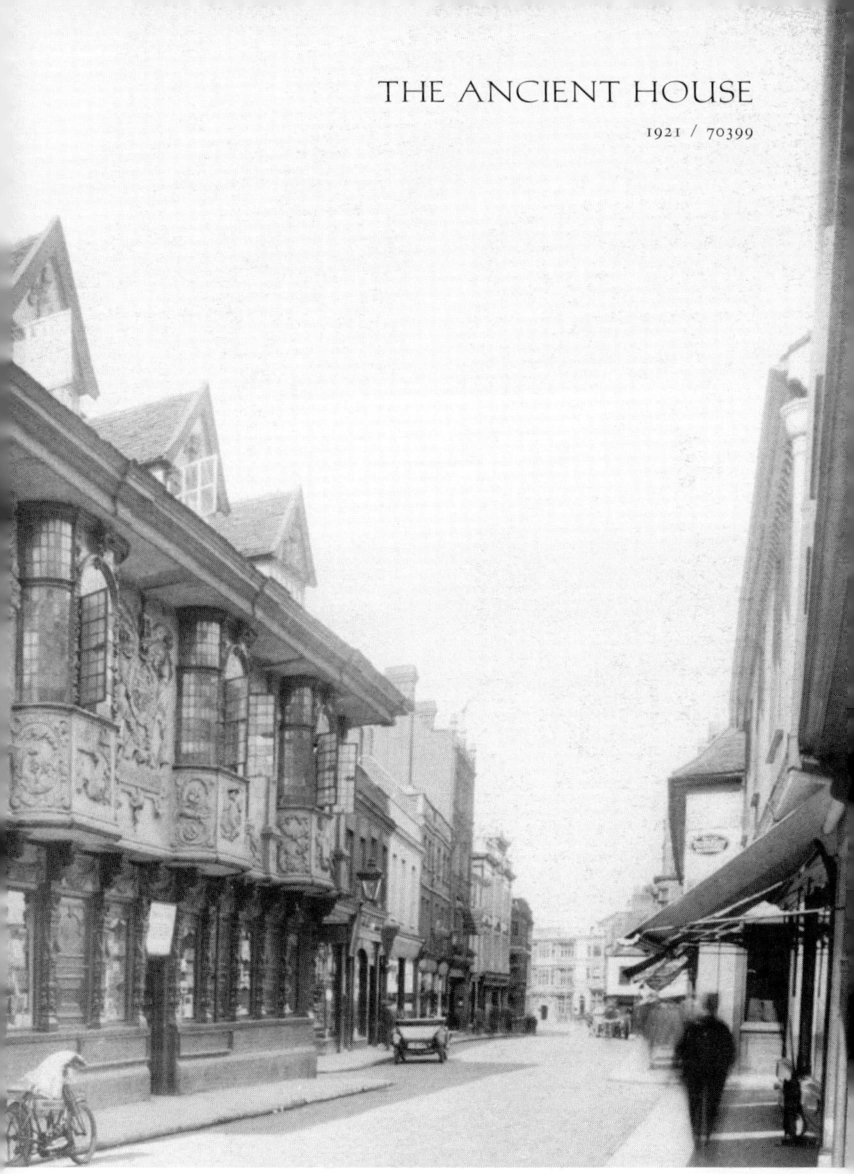

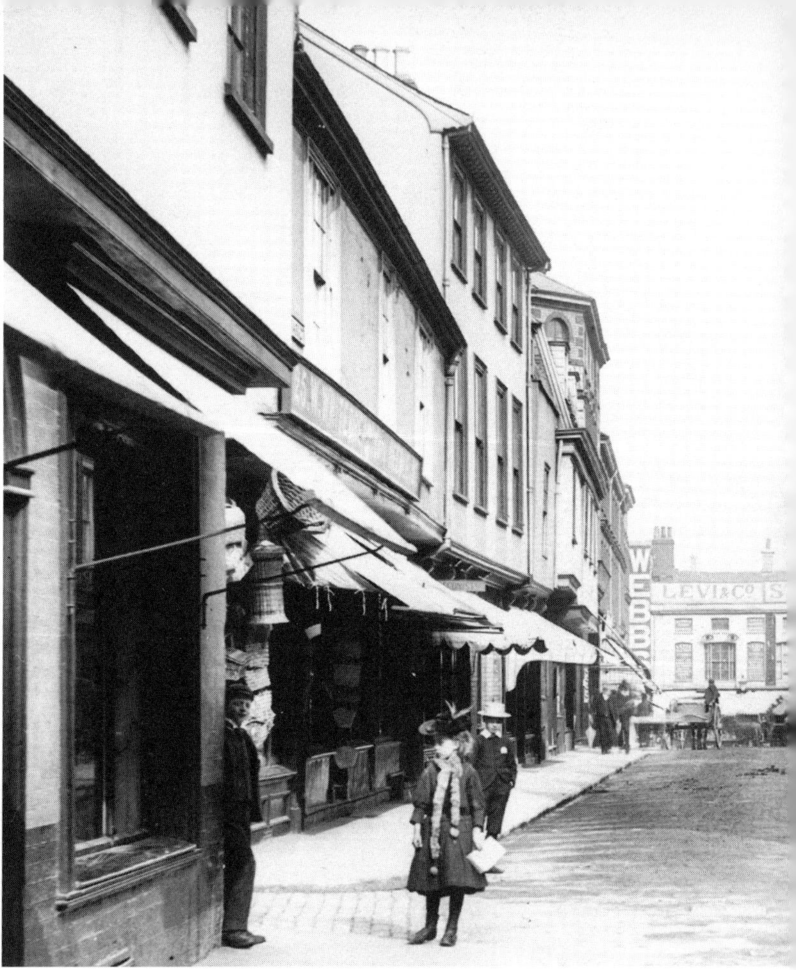

BUTTER MARKET

1893 / 32204

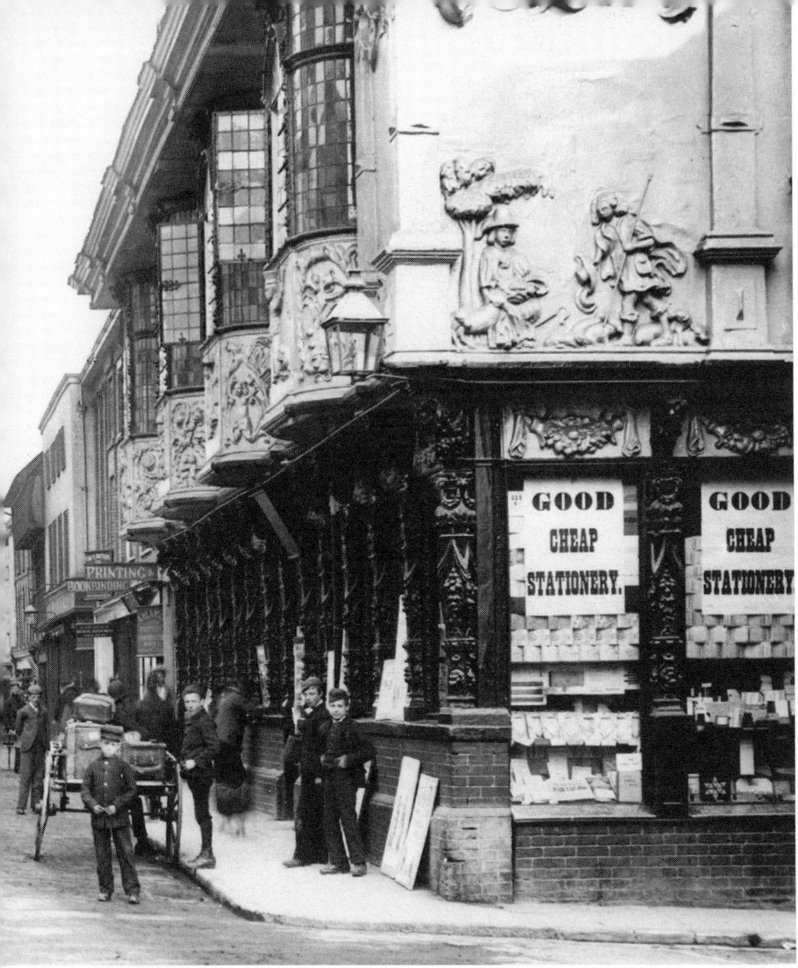

This is without doubt the best-known building in Ipswich: the Ancient House (or Sparrowe's House) and its incredible plasterwork. It was around 1670 that Robert Sparrowe remodelled the building, with the pargetting reflecting his interest in the known world at that time - the four continents of Europe, Africa, Asia and America.

Another view showing the elaborate pargetting which has made the Ancient House recognised as one of the prime examples of its kind. At the cinema next door, 'Easter Parade' is enjoying yet another re-run, with seats priced at 2/9 and 3/6 (14p and 17 ½p).

THE ANCIENT HOUSE

C1955 / 118017

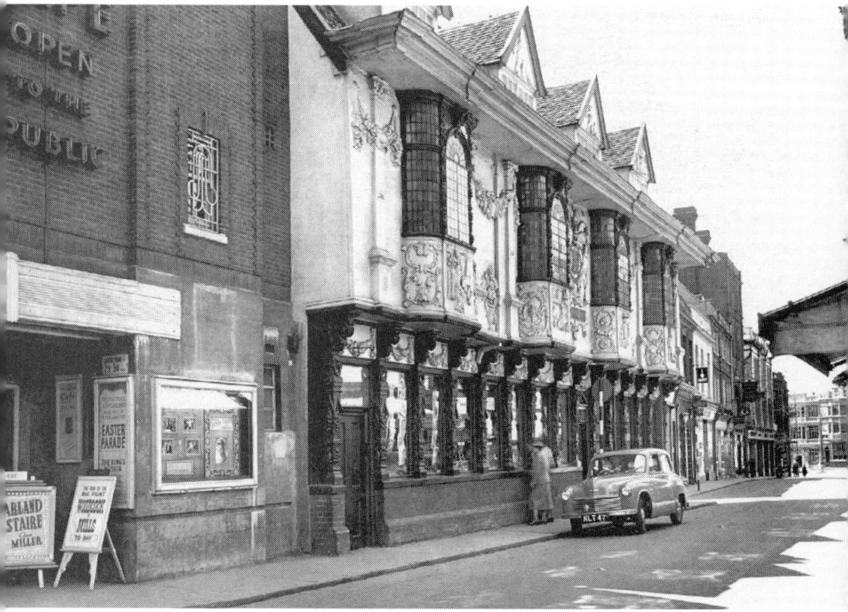

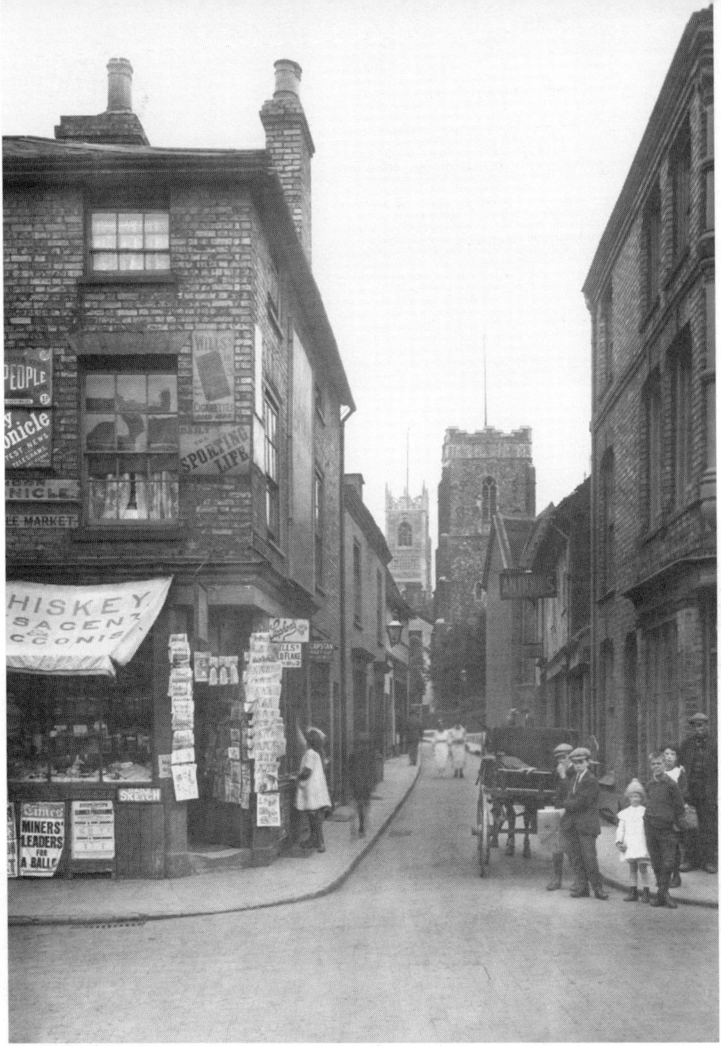

ST STEPHENS LANE

1921 / 70391

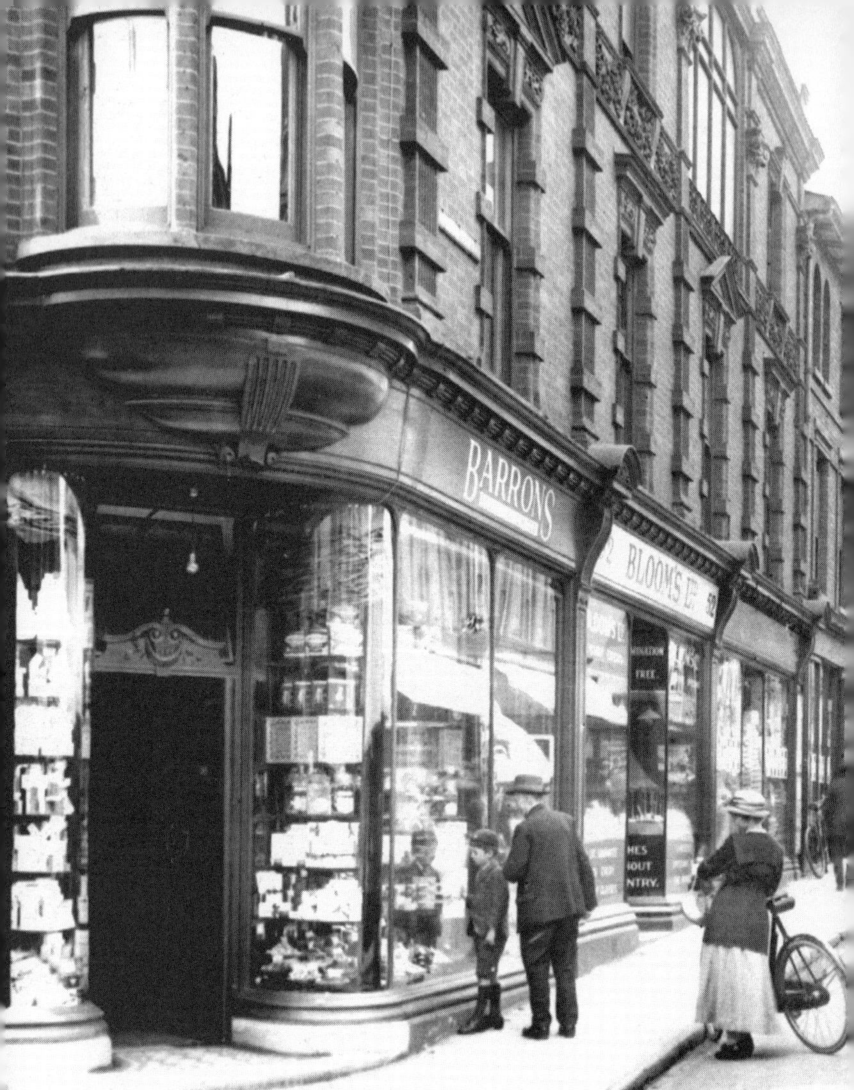
BARRONS
BLOOM'S

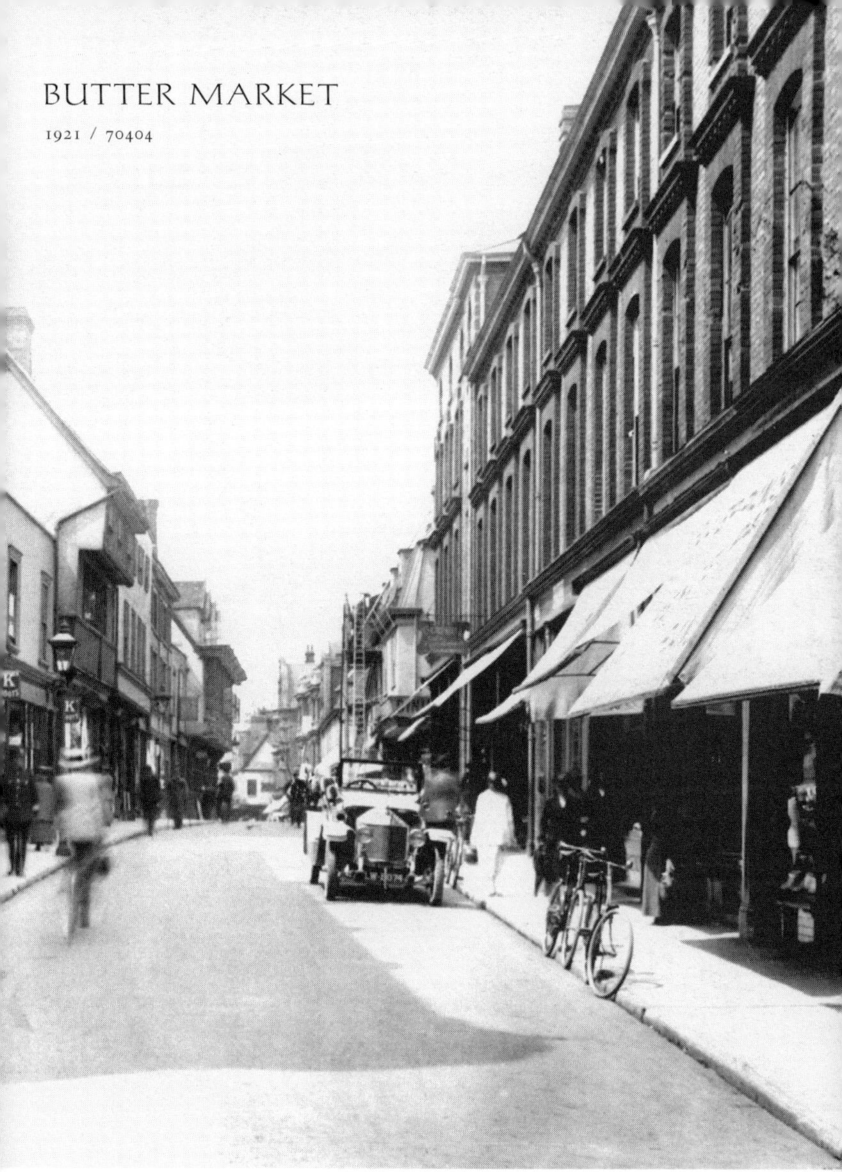

BUTTER MARKET

1921 / 70404

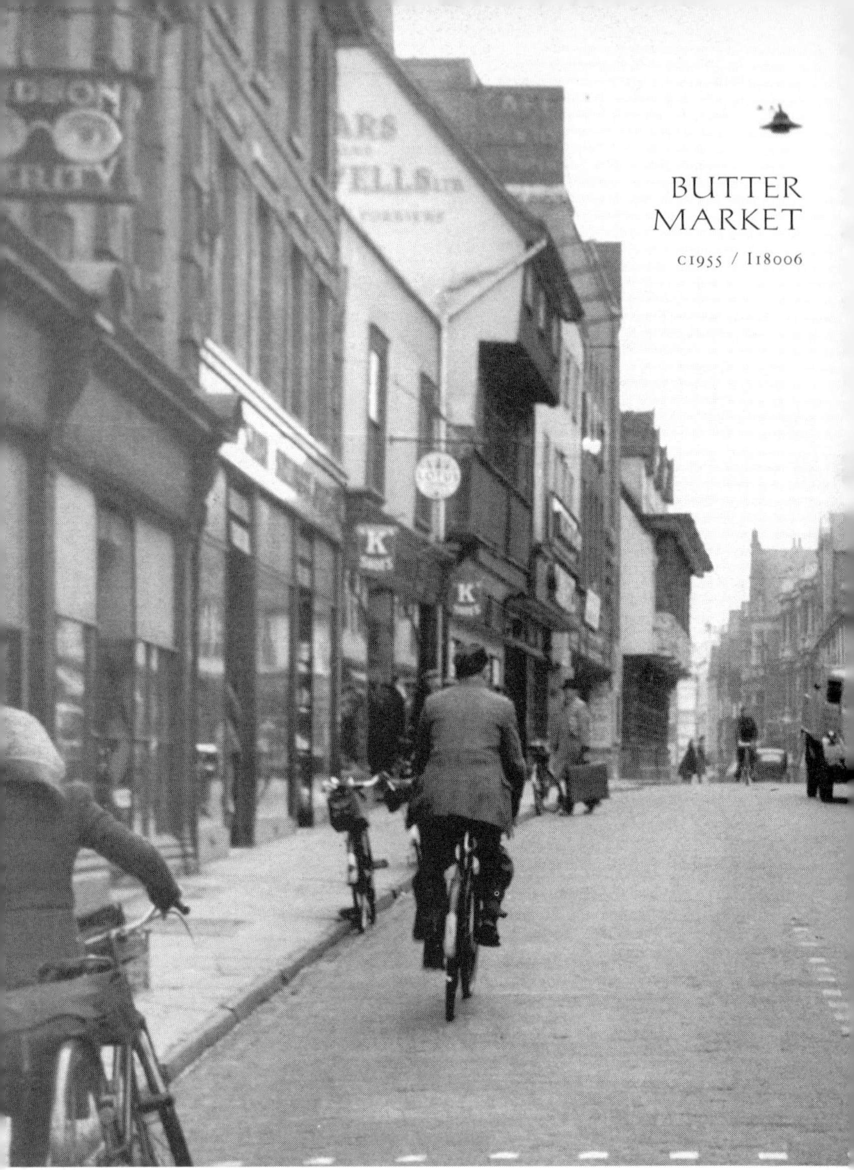

BUTTER MARKET

c1955 / I18006

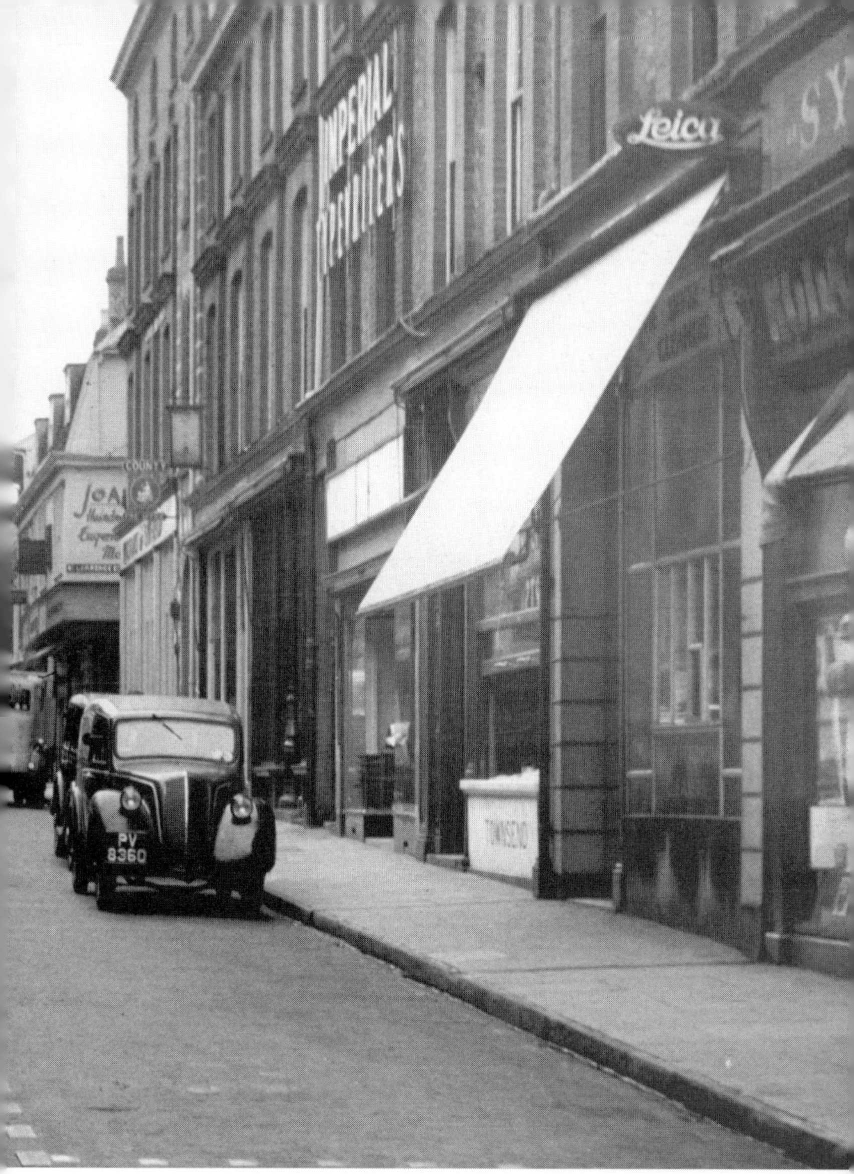
IMPERIAL
TYPEWRITERS
Leica
COUNTY
TOWNSEND
PV
8360

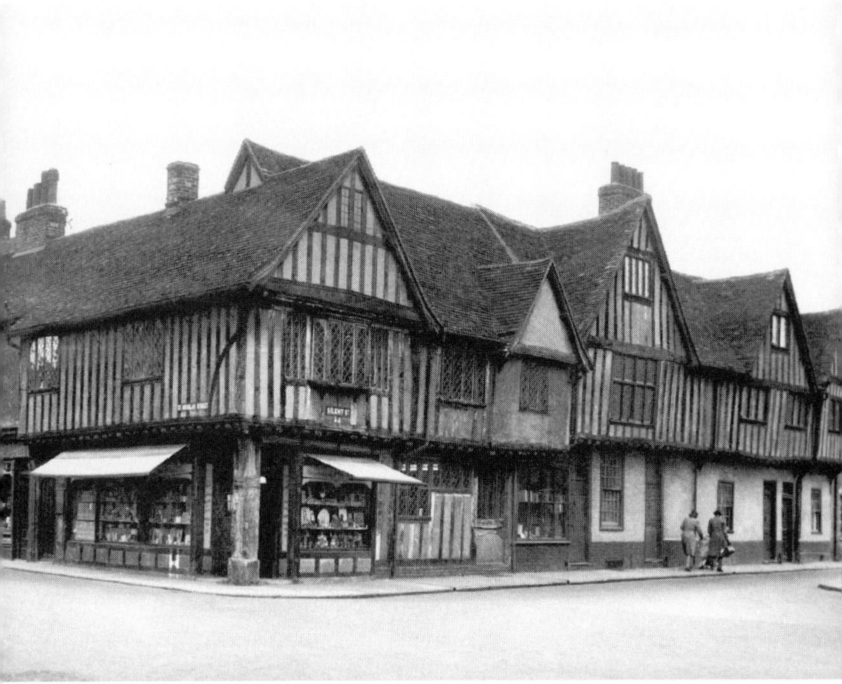

On the corner of Silent Street and St Nicholas' Street we see this impressive group of Tudor buildings with a carved corner post. Cardinal Wolsey is reputed to have been born here.

WOLSEY'S BIRTHPLACE, SILENT STREET

C1955 / I18047

The East Suffolk Hospital was founded in 1835, starting out as a two-storey building. It was extended upwards in 1869, and a children's wing was added some five years later.

THE HOSPITAL

1893 / 32216

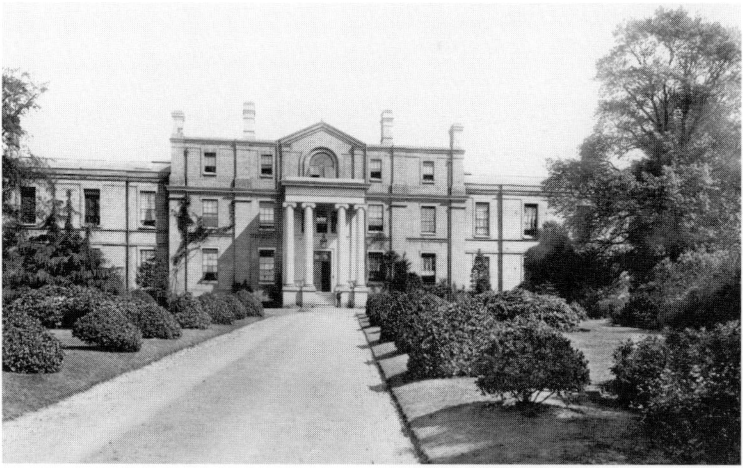

Founded in 1847, Ipswich's museum was very much aimed at educating the working classes. In 1881, this new museum, designed by Horace Cheston, was built in the High Street.

THE MUSEUM

1896 / 37309

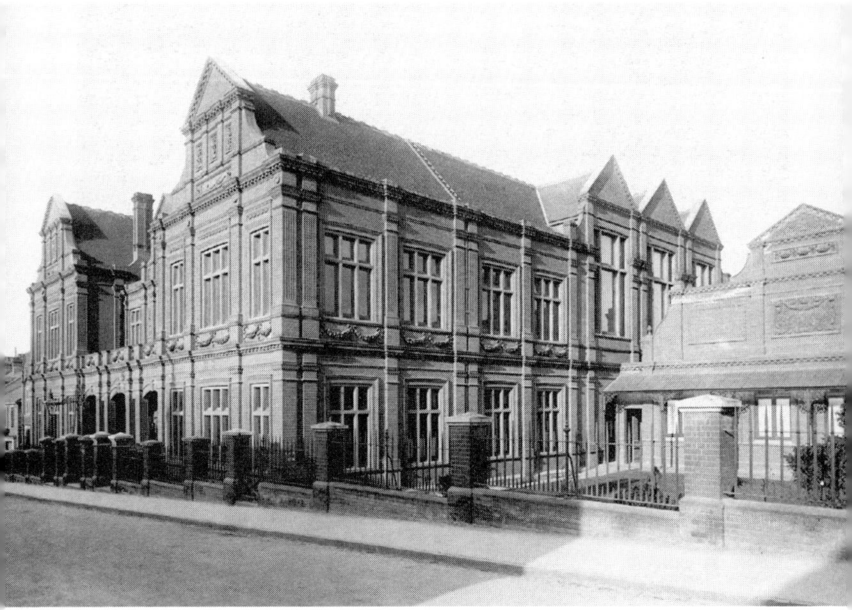

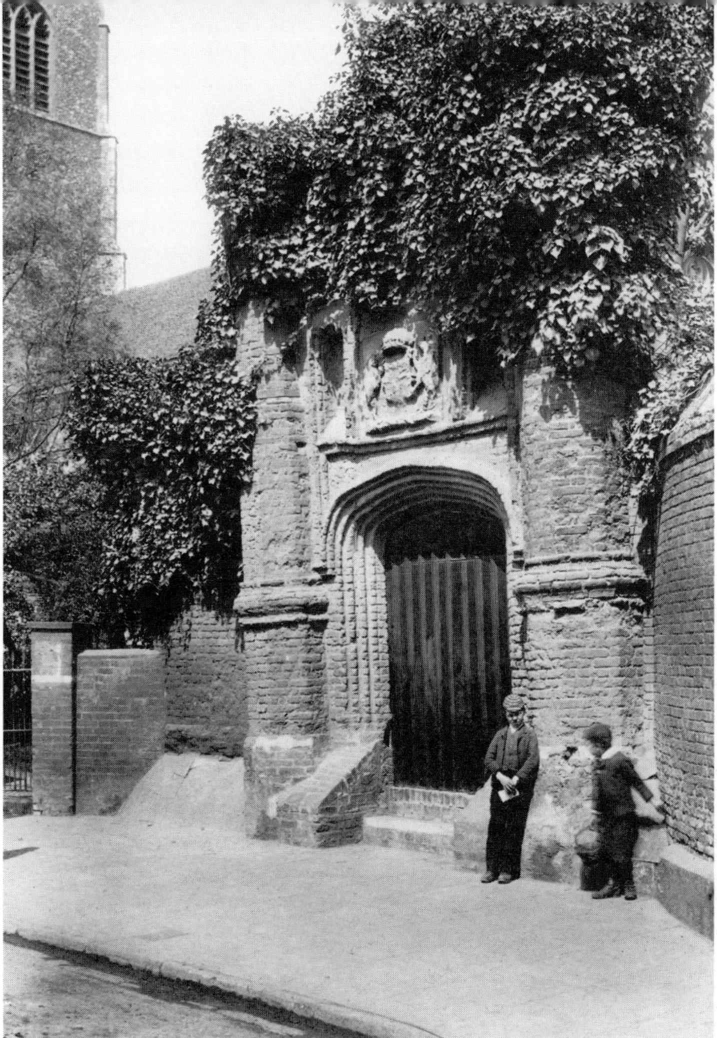

WOLSEY GATE AND
ST PETER'S CHURCH

1893 / 32218

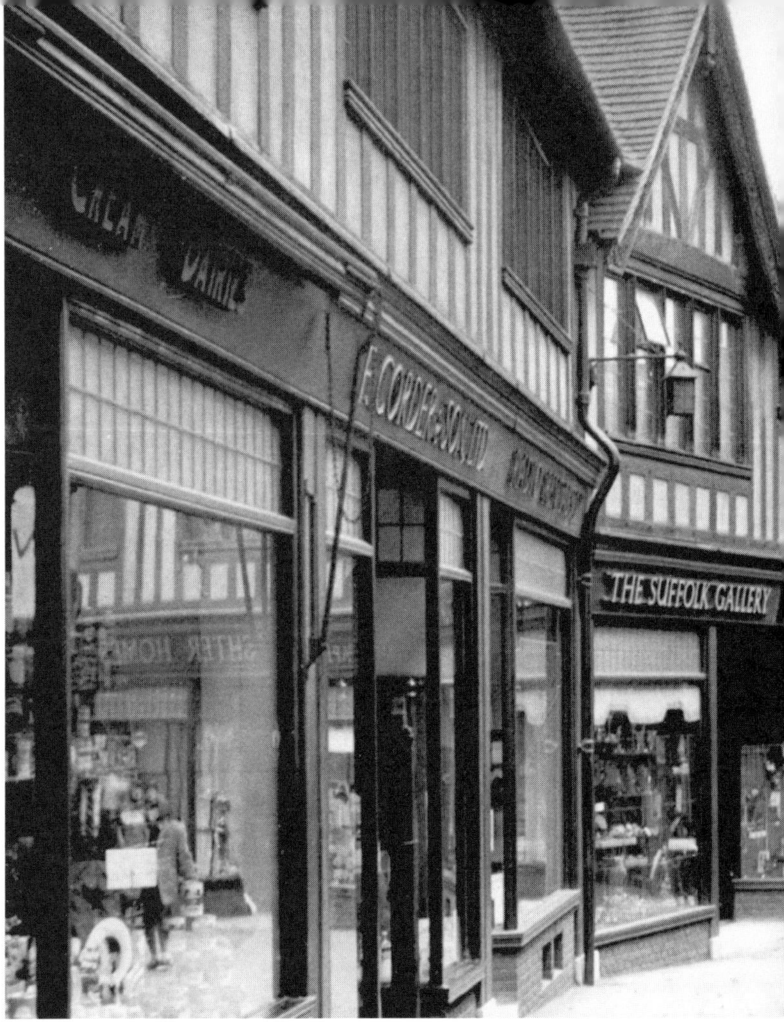

THE WALK

c1955 / I18030

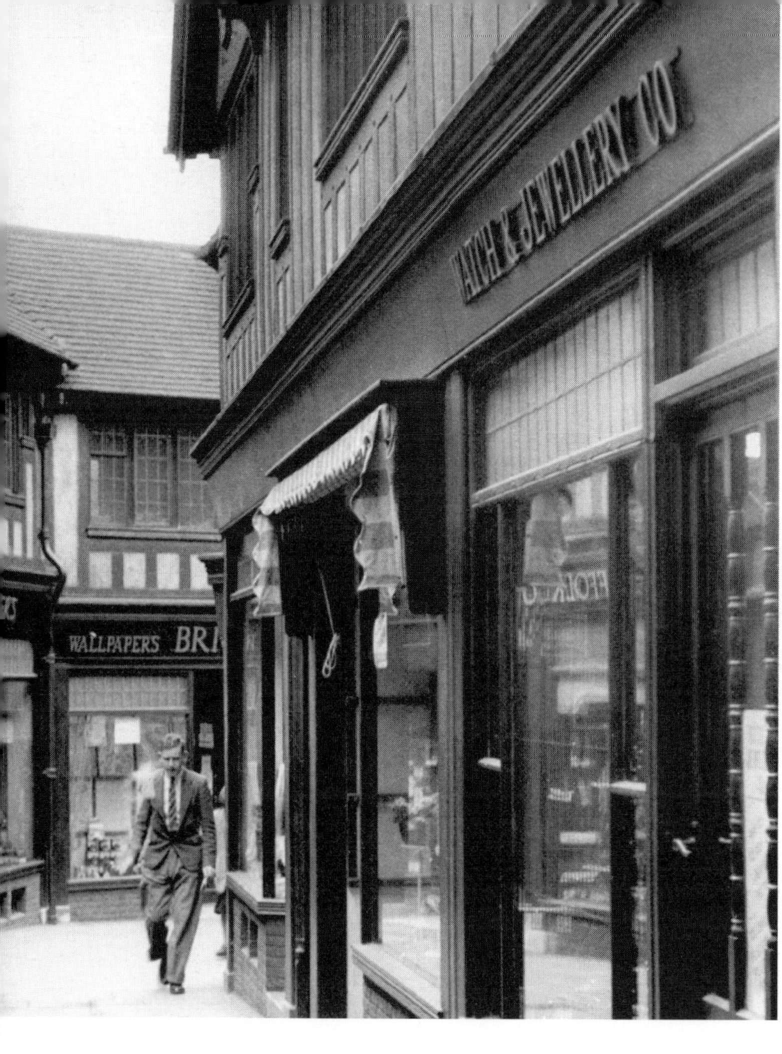

This attractive pedestrian precinct is just off Tavern Street. Although the feel is Tudor, the straightness of the lines says otherwise. The Walk was actually built in the 1930s.

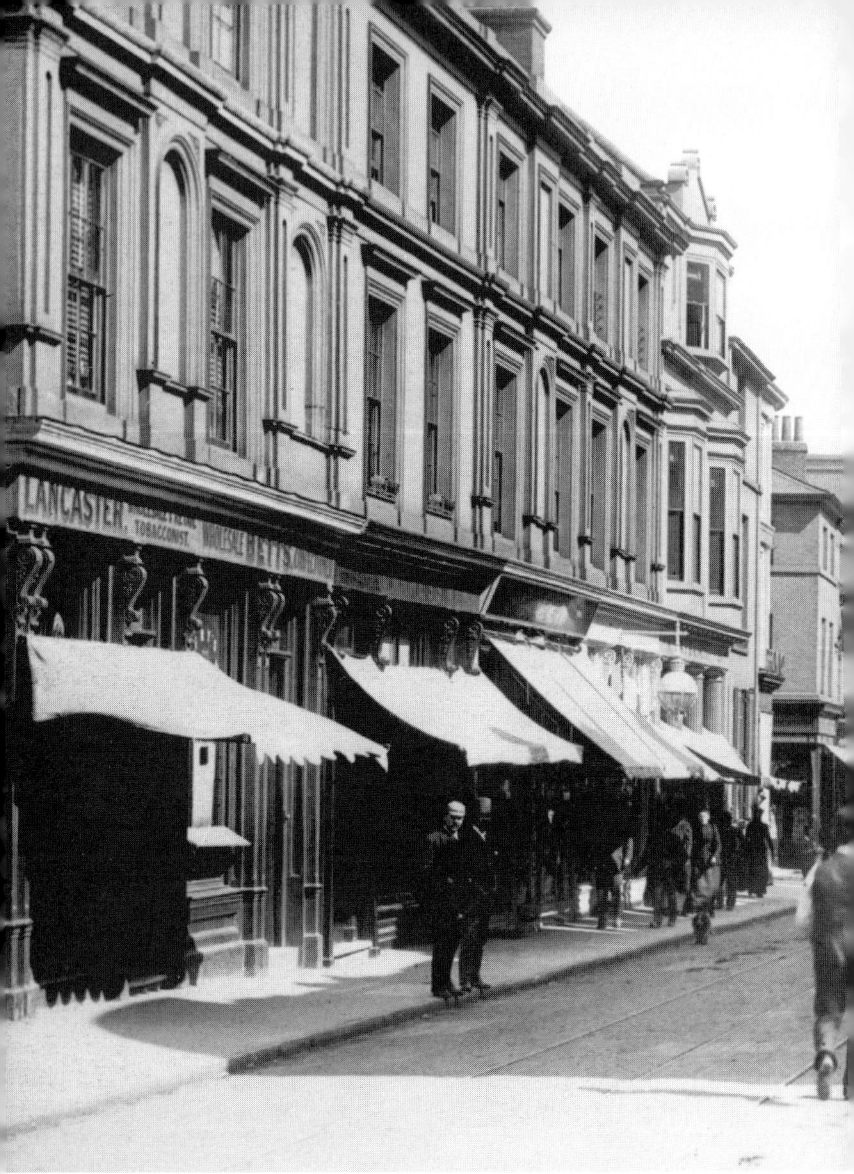
LANCASTER,
TOBACCONIST

WESTGATE STREET

1893 / 32201

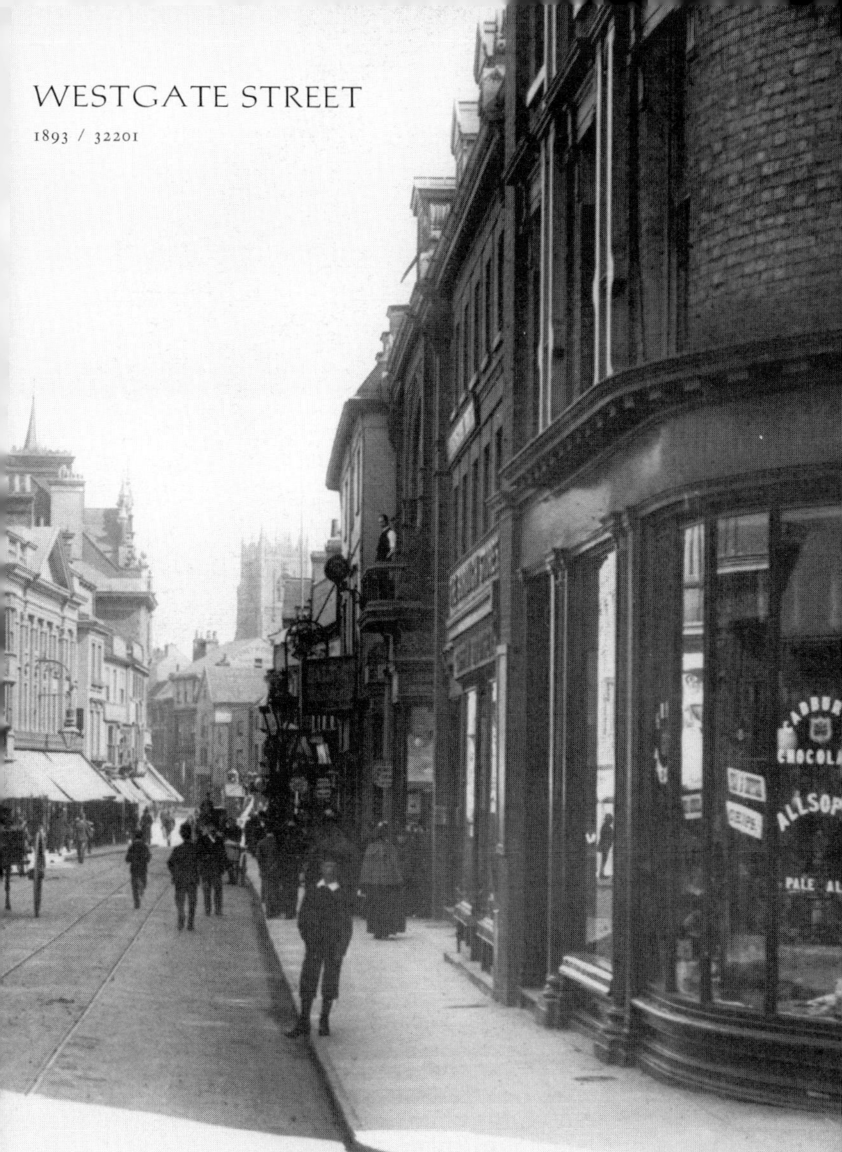

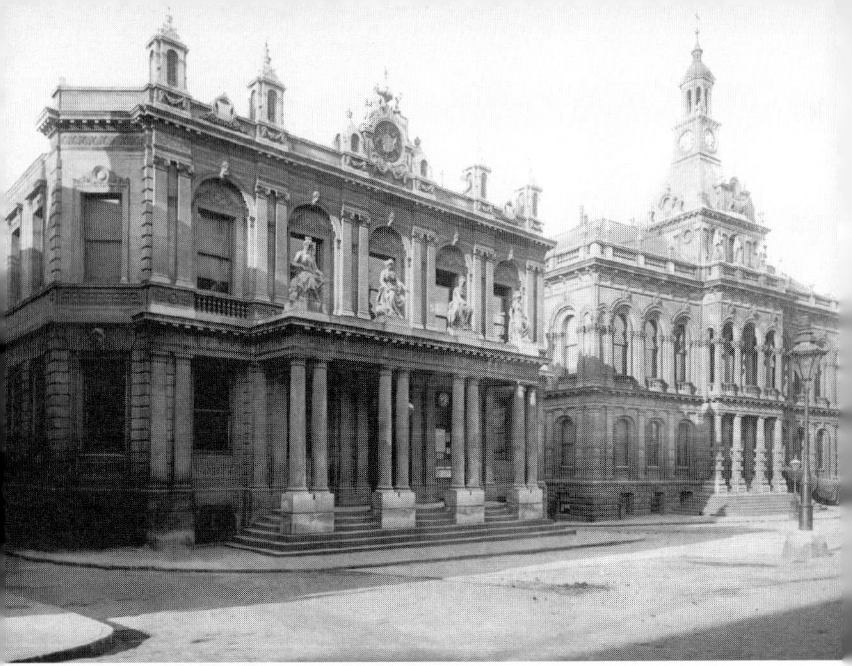

These two imposing buildings stand on Cornhill. On the left is the Post Office, built just five years previously, with its four statues representing Industry, Electricity, Steam and Commerce. To the right is the Italianate-style town hall, erected in 1867.

THE TOWN HALL AND THE POST OFFICE

1896 / 37307

THE TOWN HALL

C1955 / I18053

It is some sixty years after photograph No 37307, and while the fabric, and indeed usage, of the buildings remains pretty much the same, gas lamps have given way to electric street lights and power lines - and of course the ubiquitous motor car is making its presence felt.

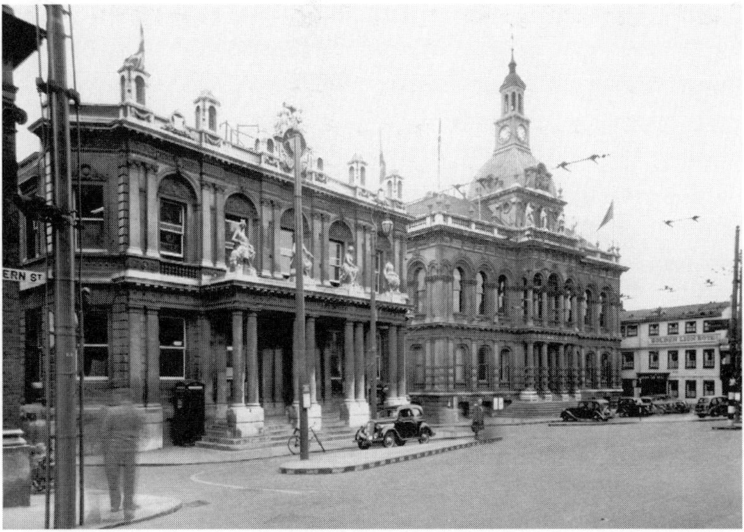

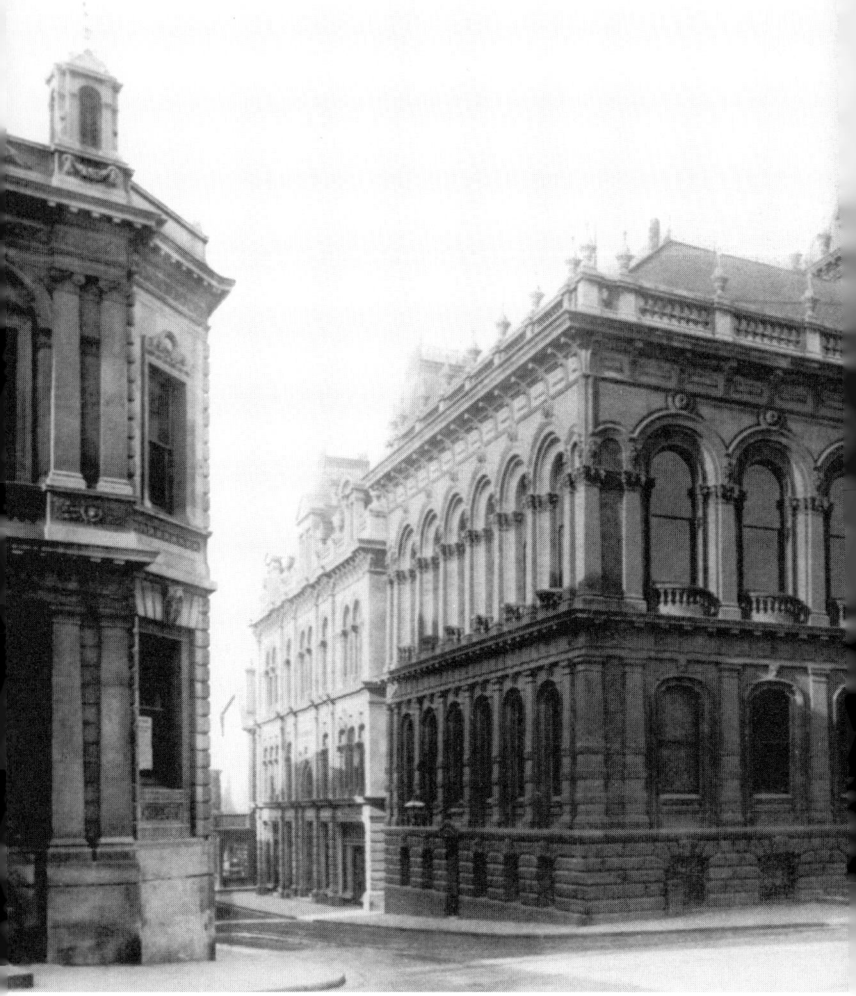

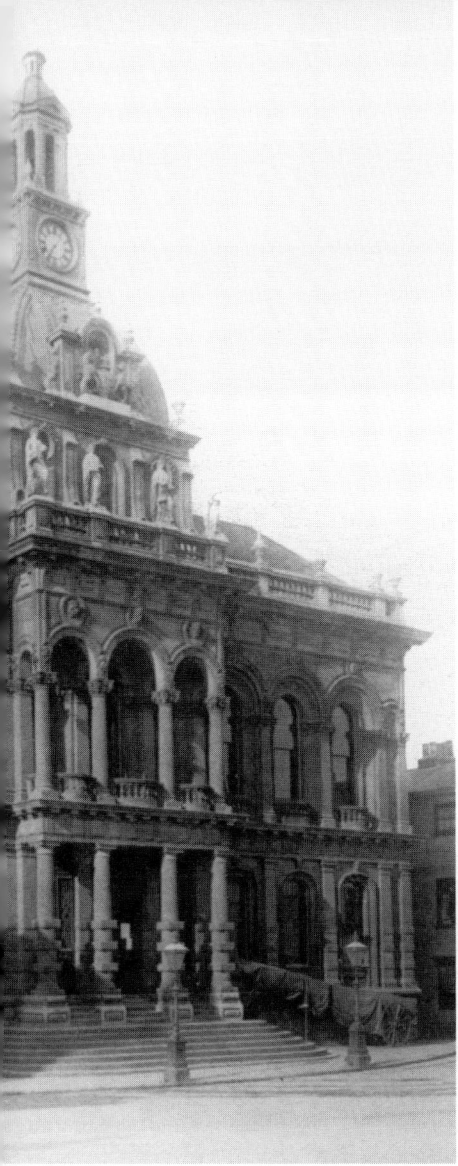

This photograph lets us have a closer look at the Venetian-style town hall standing on Cornhill. The four figures below the clock represent Commerce, Agriculture, Learning and Justice.

THE TOWN HALL

1896 / 37308

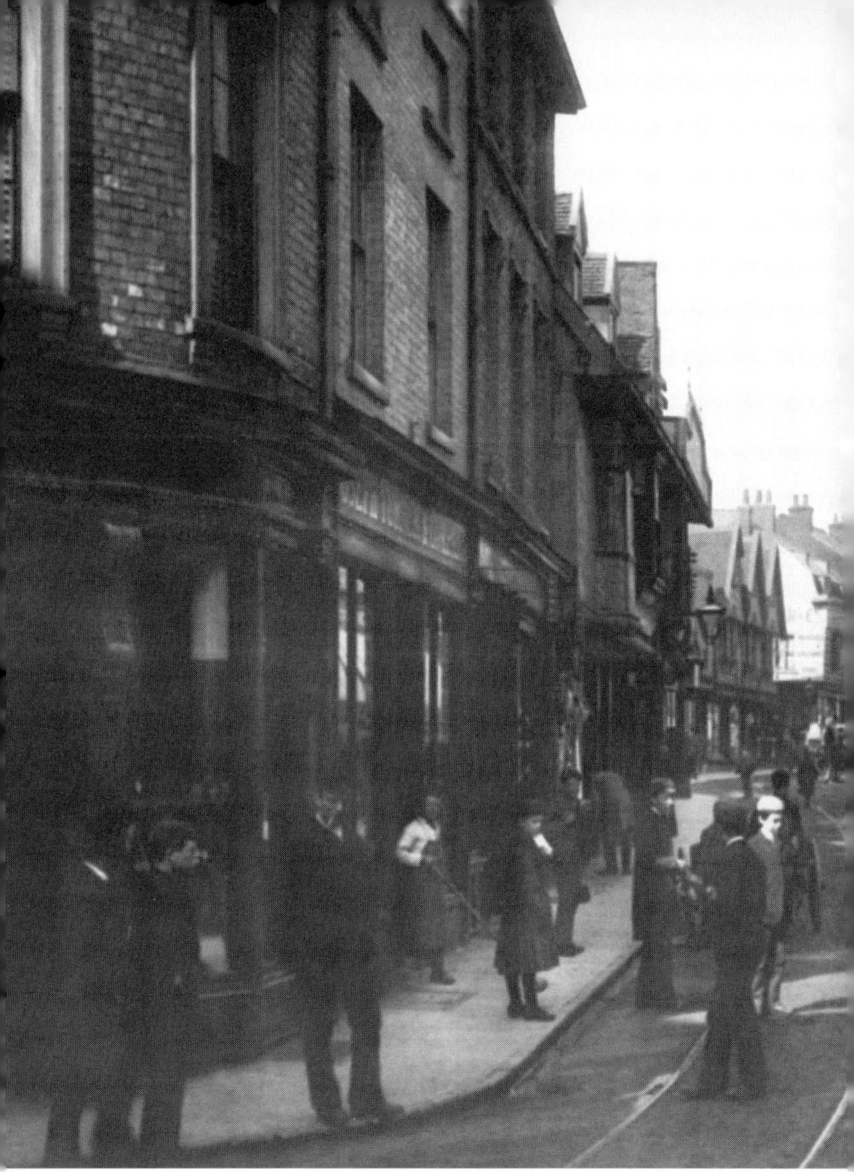

THE WHITE HORSE

1893 / 32202

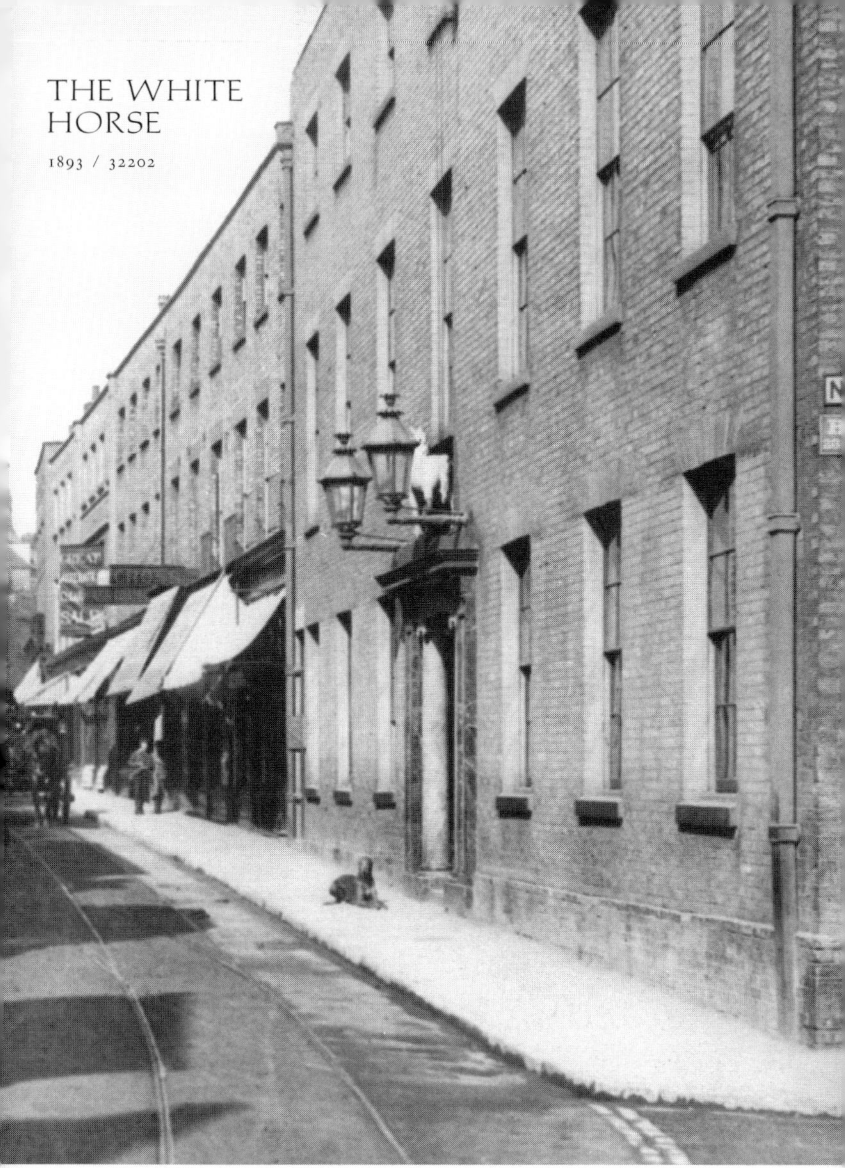

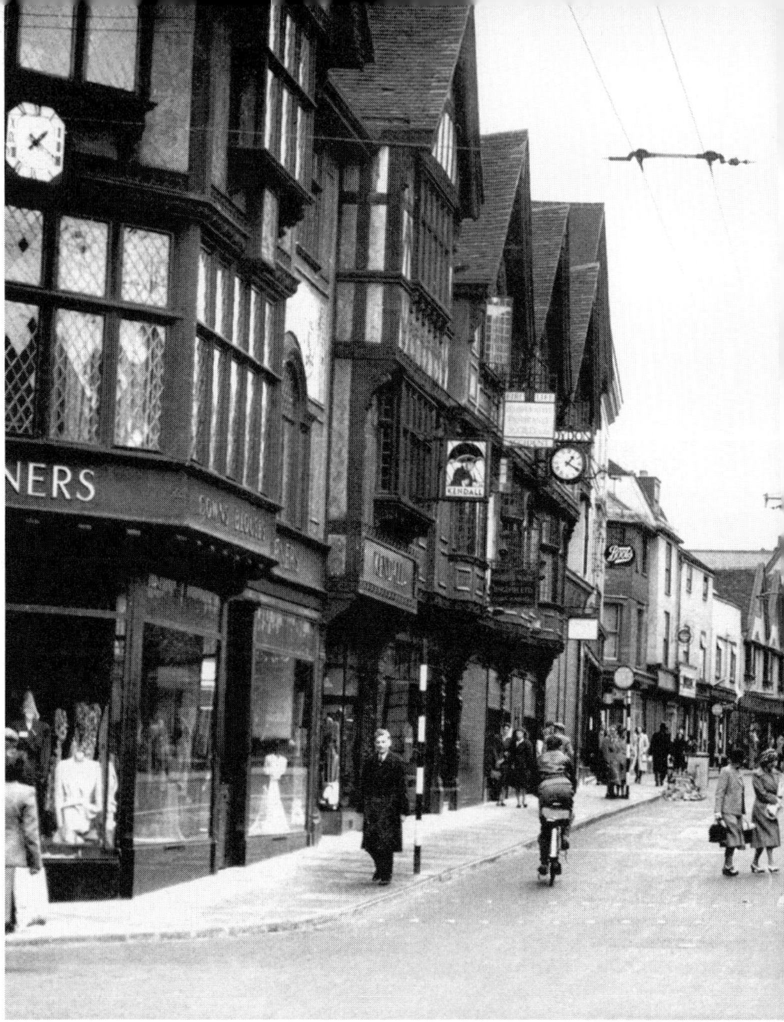

TAVERN STREET

C1955 / I18036

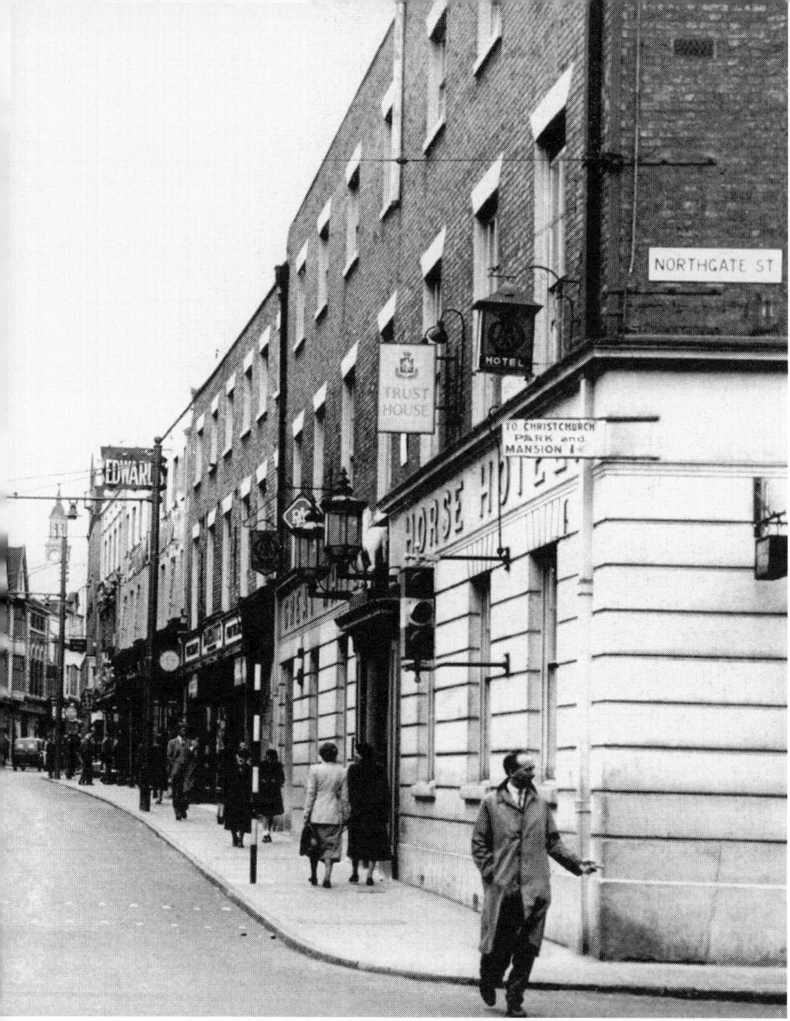

It is over sixty years after photograph No 32202, and the Great White Horse Hotel has acquired stone cladding, several signs and a set of traffic lights. Strangely, the buildings on the left look more authentically old than they did in 1893!

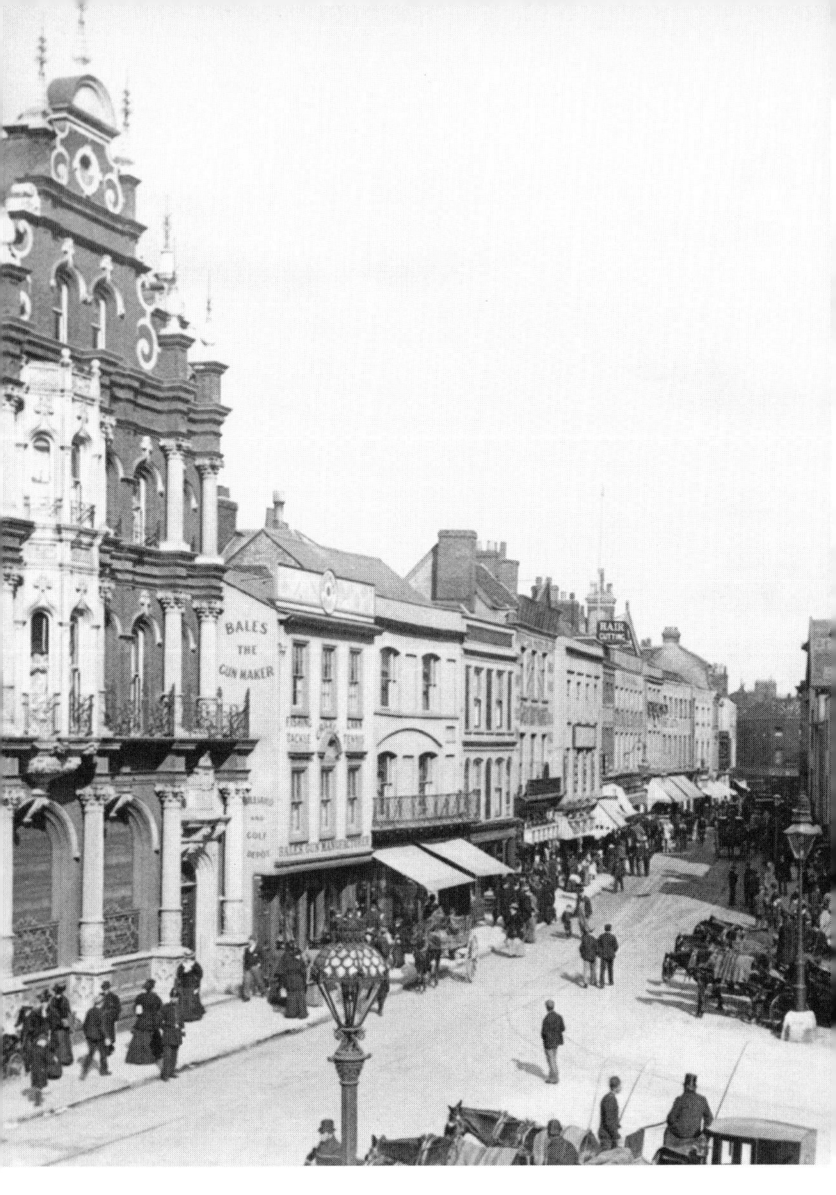
BALES
THE
GUN MAKER
HAIR CUTTING

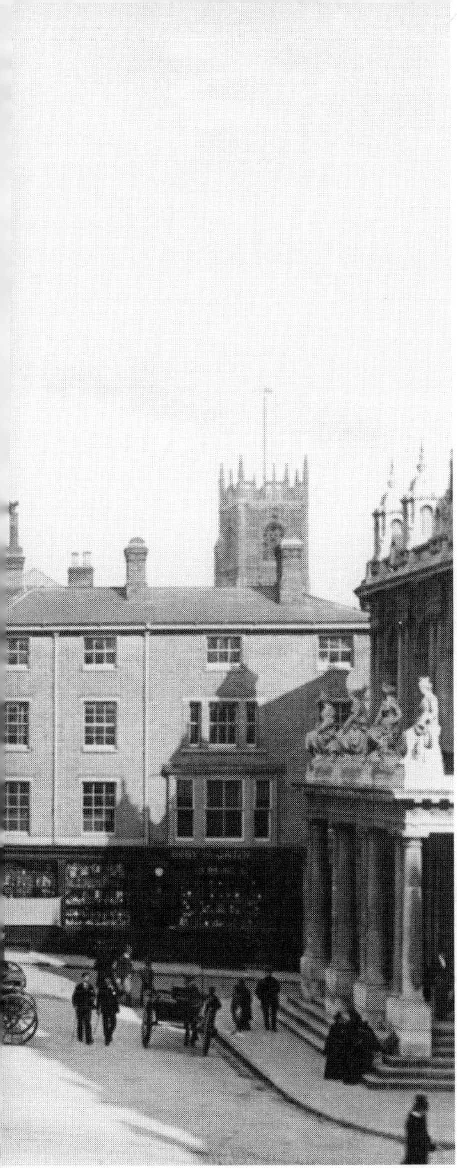

We are looking east along Tavern Street from Cornhill. On the left is the red brick and stone Lloyds Bank building, with its fretted skyline, while to the right is the neo-classical Post Office, built in 1881.

TAVERN STREET

1896 / 37306

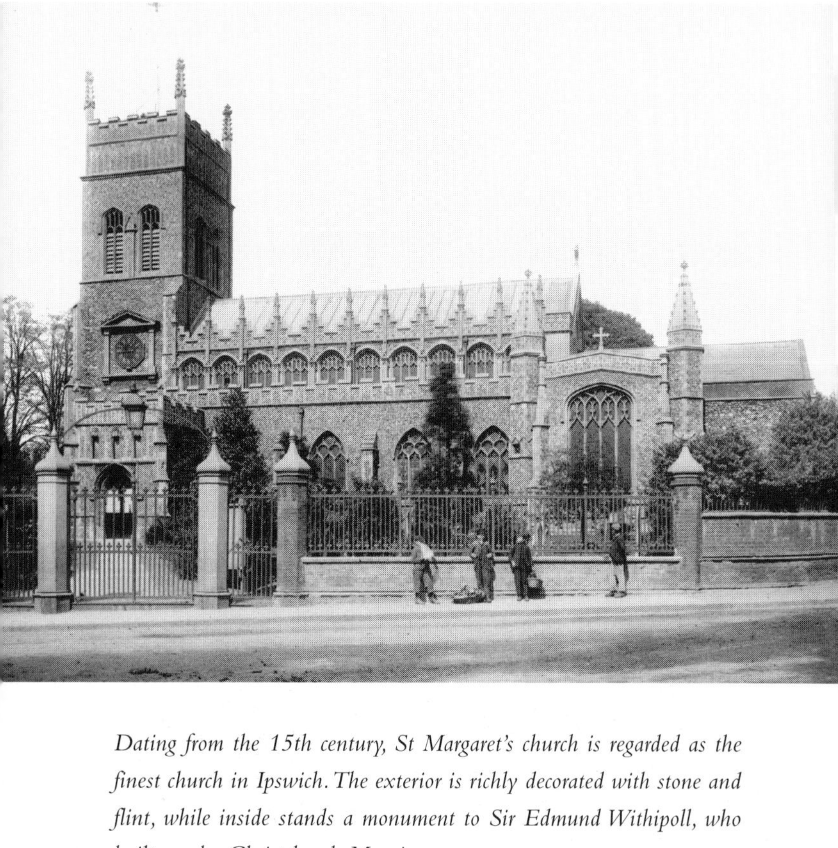

Dating from the 15th century, St Margaret's church is regarded as the finest church in Ipswich. The exterior is richly decorated with stone and flint, while inside stands a monument to Sir Edmund Withipoll, who built nearby Christchurch Mansion.

ST MARGARET'S CHURCH

1893 / 32220

This group of Tudor houses was originally plastered, and before a road-widening scheme in 1931, three gables stood across the St Margaret's Plain end. The timberwork was exposed as part of the reconstruction after much of the building was demolished.

OLD HOUSES ST MARGARET'S PLAIN

C1955 / I18045

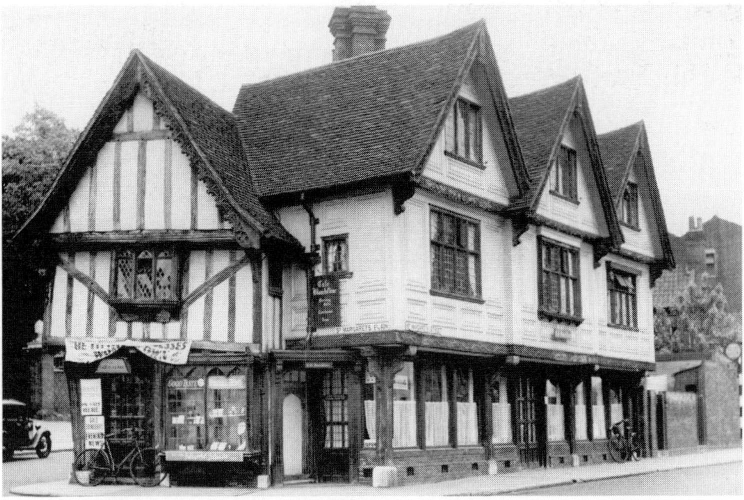

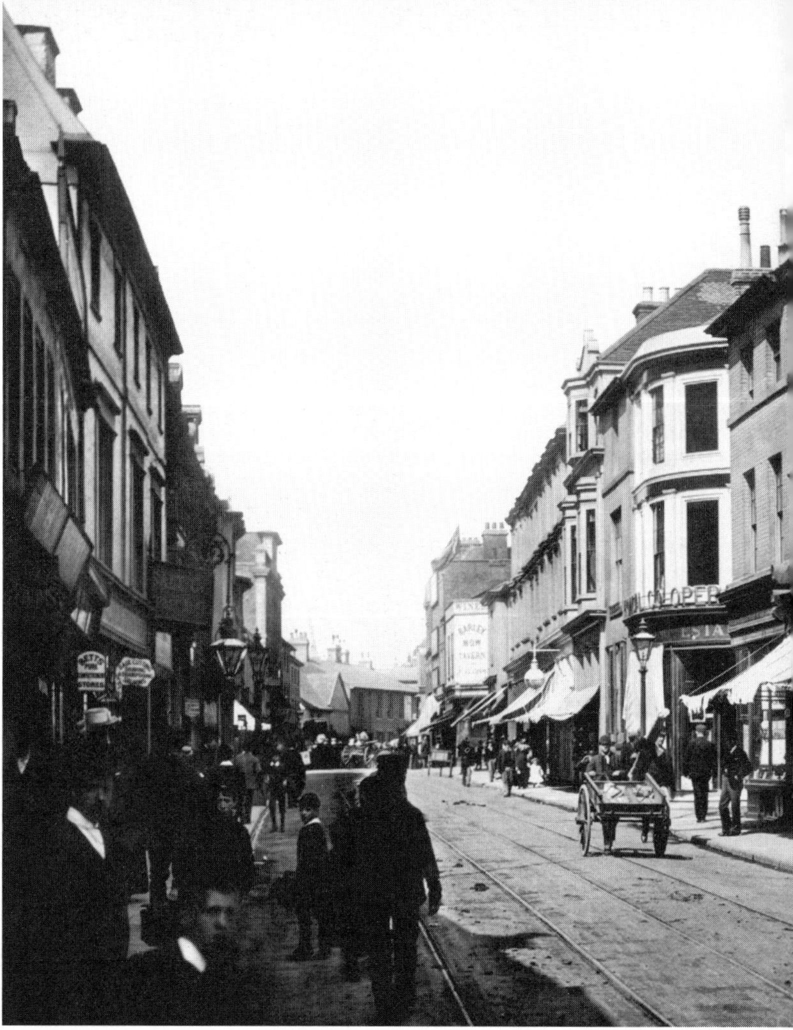

WESTGATE STREET

1893 / 32200

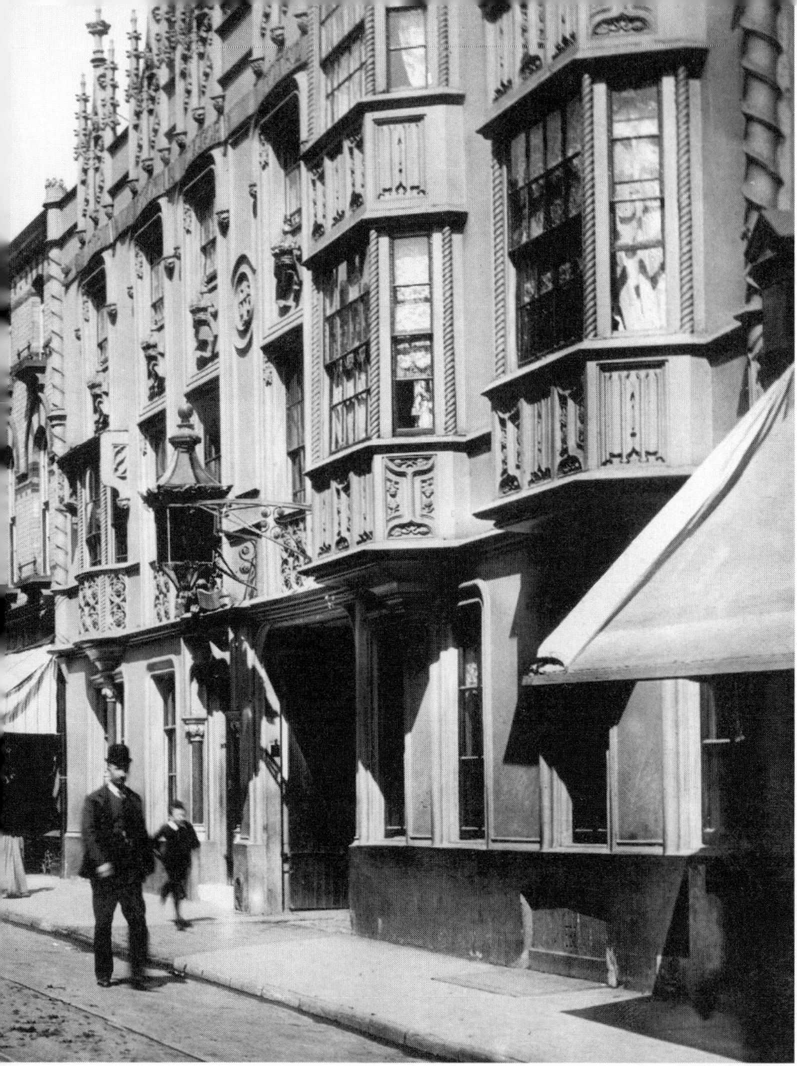

The name of the street harks back to the days of the medieval walled town. The gate itself was demolished in 1781.

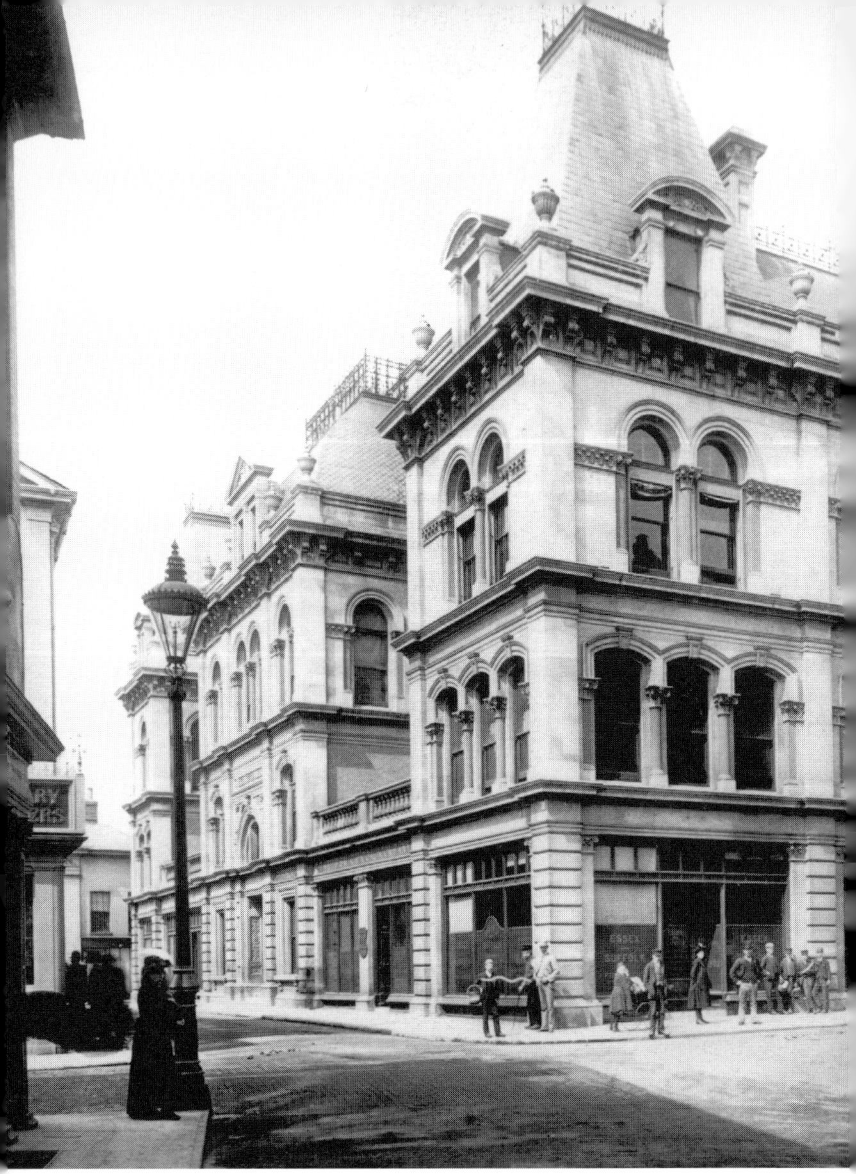

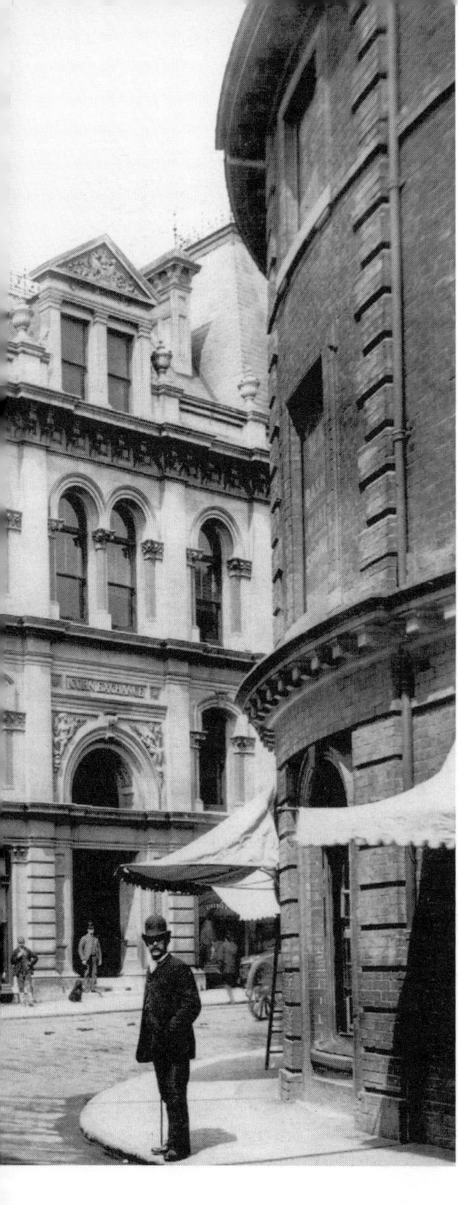

Built in 1882, the Corn Exchange continued in use as such right up until 1972. Back in the days when taking a picture involved a large and unwieldy camera and tripod, a photographer tended to attract a good deal of attention, but at least there appear to be plenty of people to hand willing to co-operate.

THE CORN EXCHANGE

1893 / 32203

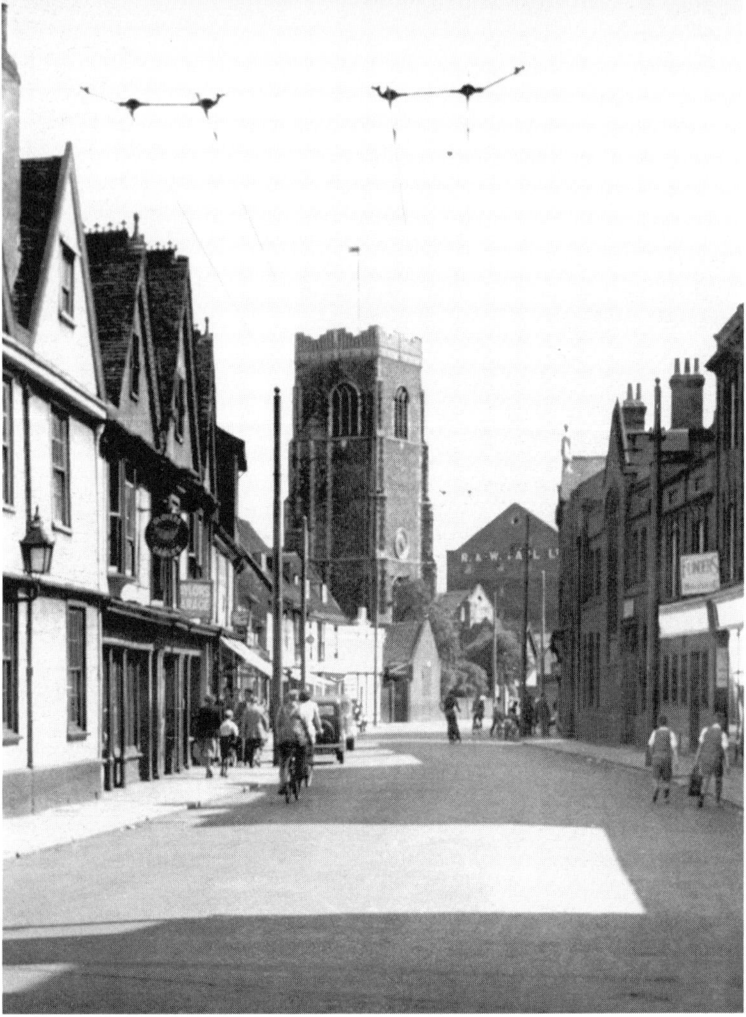

ST PETER'S STREET

C1955 / I18022

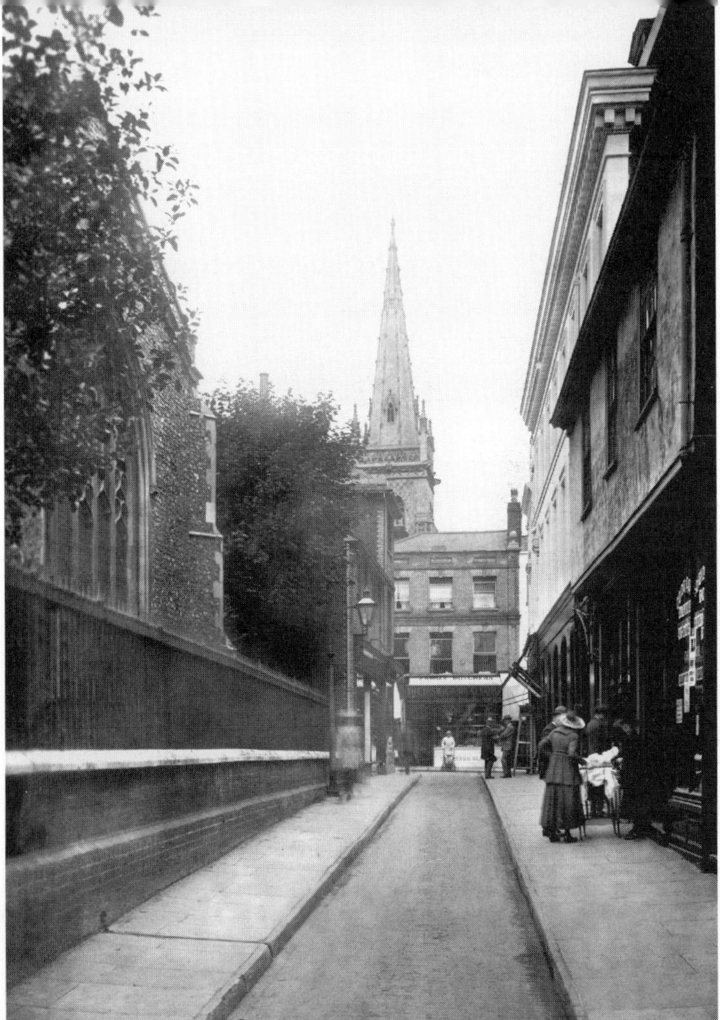

ST LAWRENCE STREET

1921 / 70389

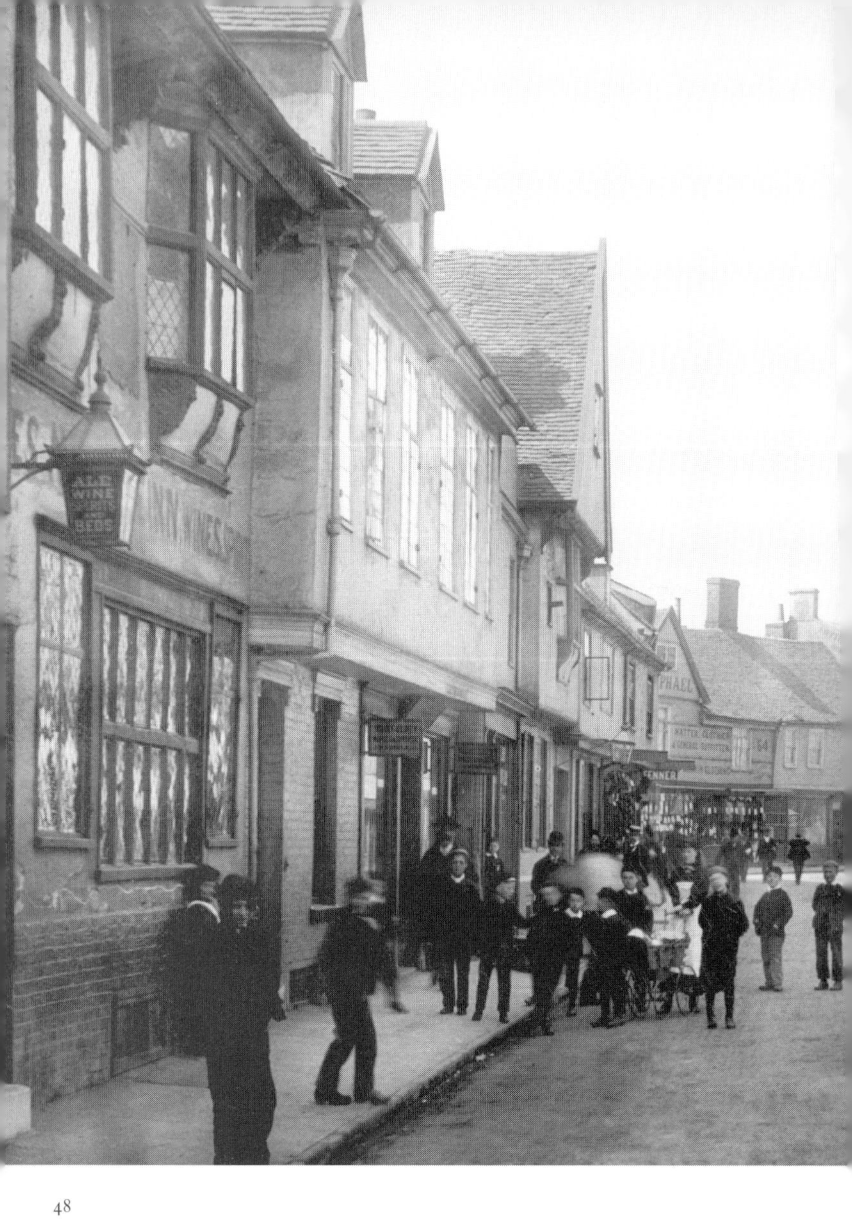
WINE
BEDS
FENNER
64

FORE STREET

1893 / 32206

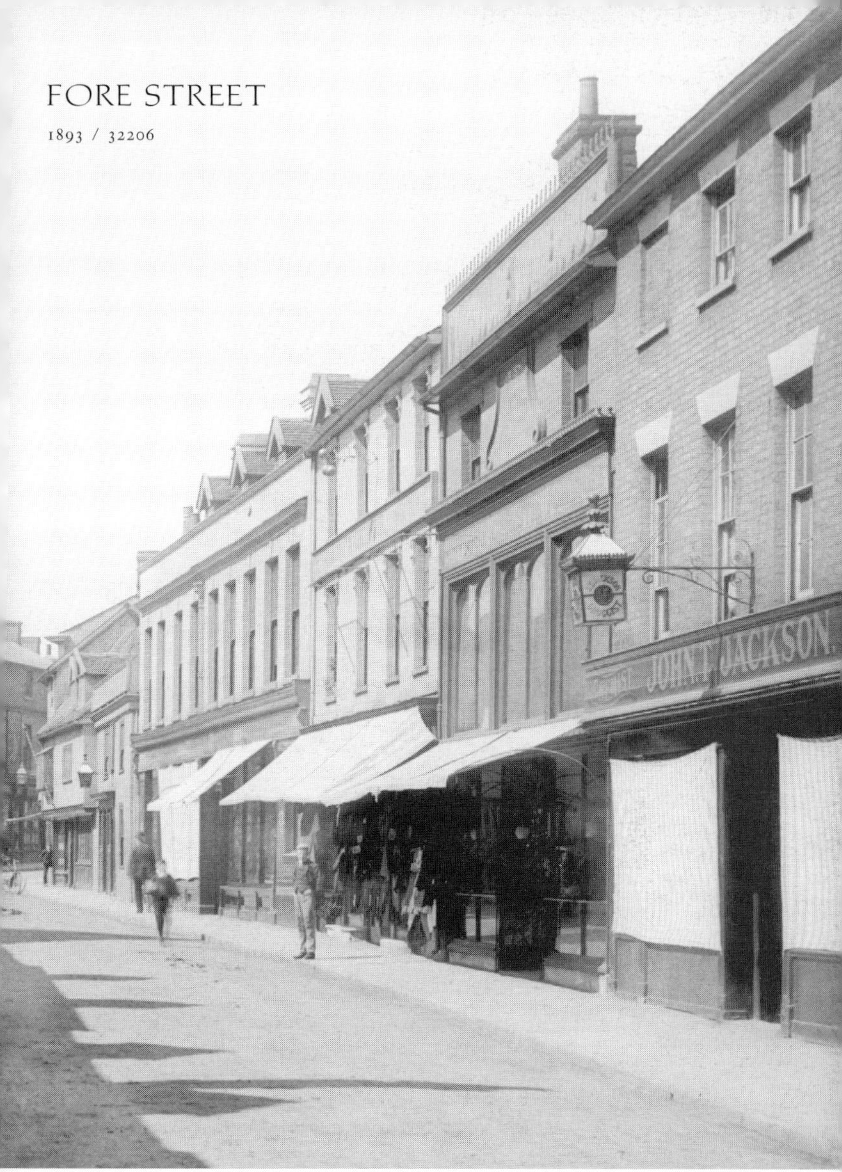

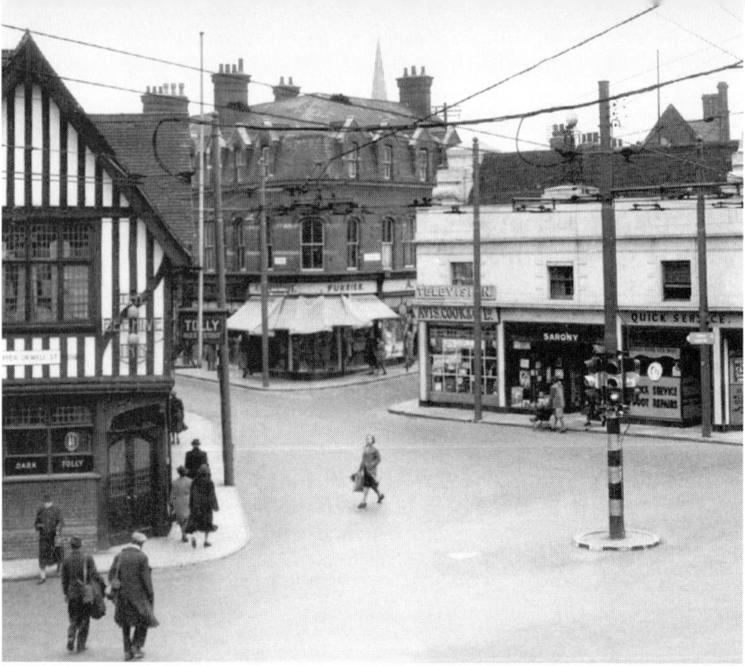

Trolley buses were still operating in Ipswich when this photo was taken, as we can see from the overhead power lines. With traffic lights in the middle of the junction at Major's Corner, and pedestrian activity reasonably busy, where, one wonders, is all the traffic?

MAJOR'S CORNER

c1955 / I18033

ELECTRIC HOUSE AND THE CAR PARK

C1955 / I18044

Electricity has played a great part in transport in Ipswich throughout the first half of the 20th century, first with trams, and then with the trolley buses. But the writing was certainly on the wall, judging from this jam-packed car park.

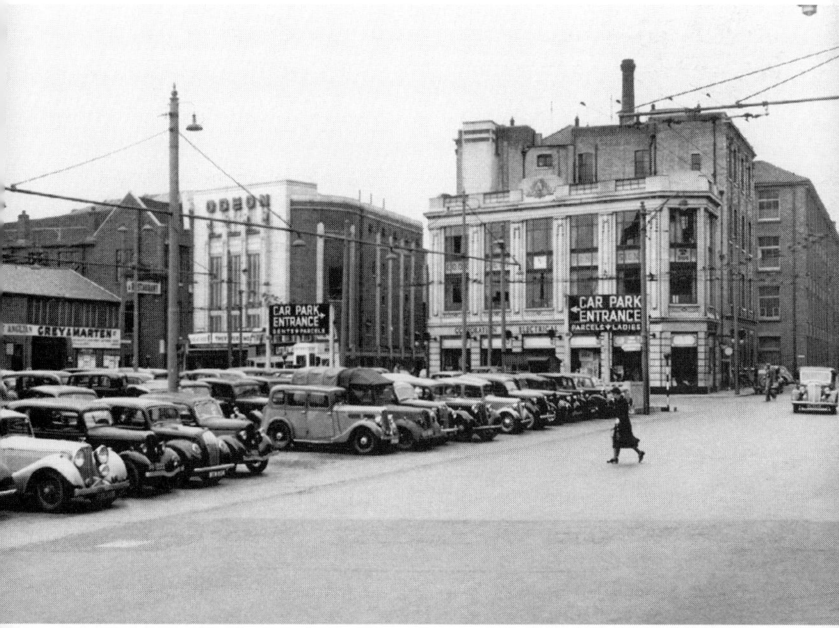

Built on the site of the 12th-century priory of the Holy Trinity, this marvellous Tudor country house almost became a housing estate in the late 19th century. The Cobbold brewing family bought the building and then presented it to the town, thus enabling us to continue to enjoy this monument to gracious living.

CHRISTCHURCH MANSION

1893 / 32217

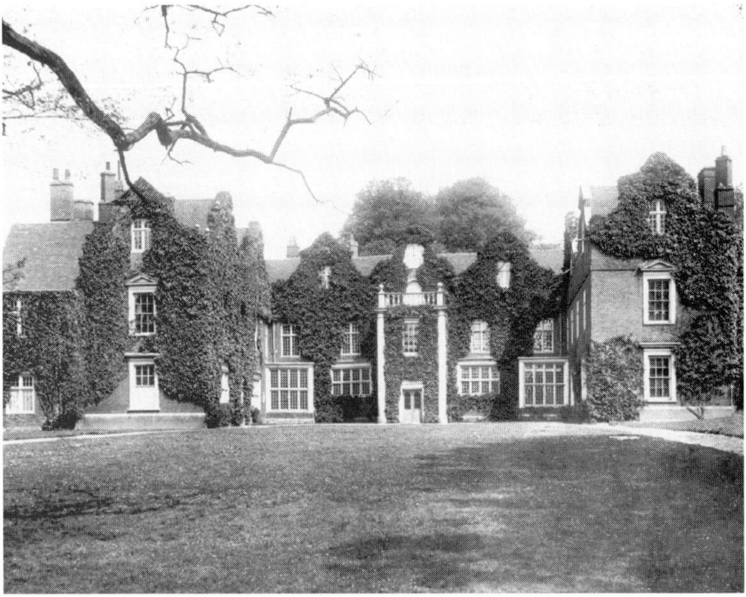

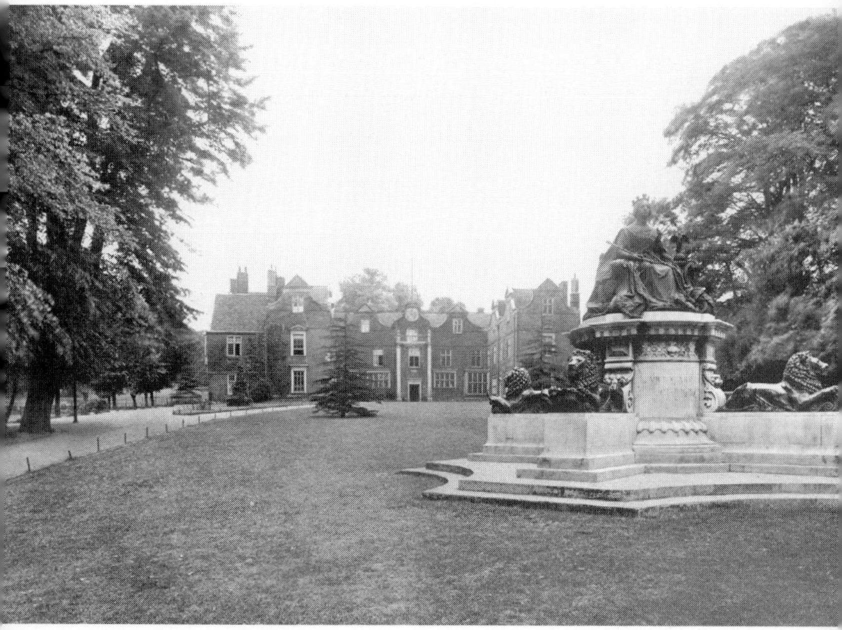

A monument to Queen Victoria stands in the park in front of the 16th-century Christchurch Mansion. Its very Dutch-looking curved and pedimented gables came when the house was rebuilt after fire destroyed the upper storey in 1674. When Daniel Defoe visited Ipswich in 1722, he commented on how many townsfolk used the park, likening its popularity to that of Kensington Gardens.

CHRISTCHURCH PARK

1921 / 70405

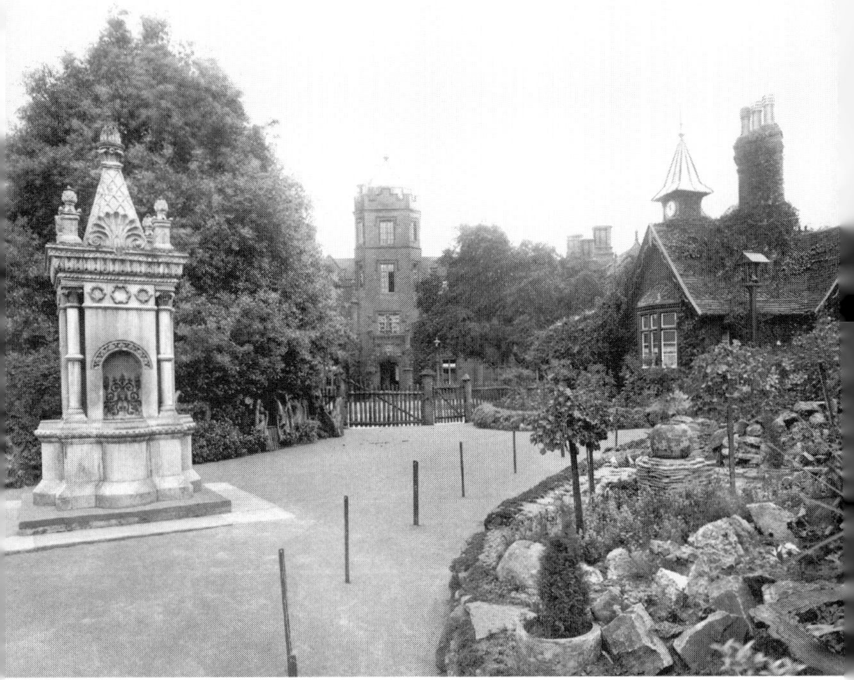

Ipswich's Grammar School was founded in the beginning of the 15th century. This particular building, designed by Christopher Fleury, was built in what was then the outskirts of town, in the mid 19th century.

THE GRAMMAR SCHOOL AND THE UPPER ARBORETUM

1921 / 70396

Here we see the beautiful ornamental gardens and the ornate drinking fountain in the arboretum adjoining the Grammar School.

THE UPPER ARBORETUM

1921 / 70397

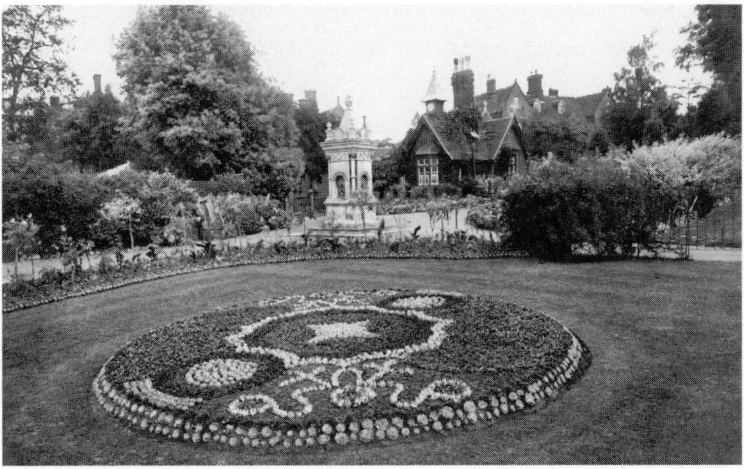

The Arboretum, adjacent to Christchurch Park, still survives, over a hundred years after this photograph was taken. These youngsters have stopped playing just long enough to stand still for the photographer.

THE LOWER ARBORETUM

1893 / 32215

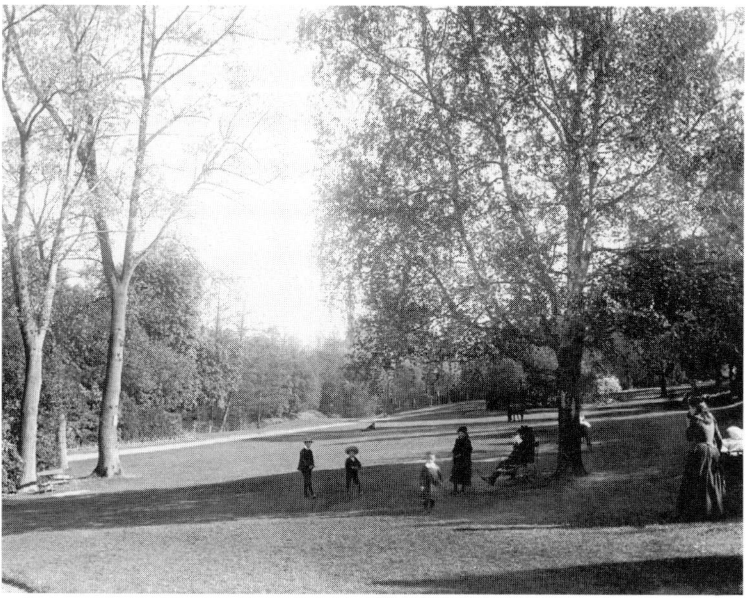

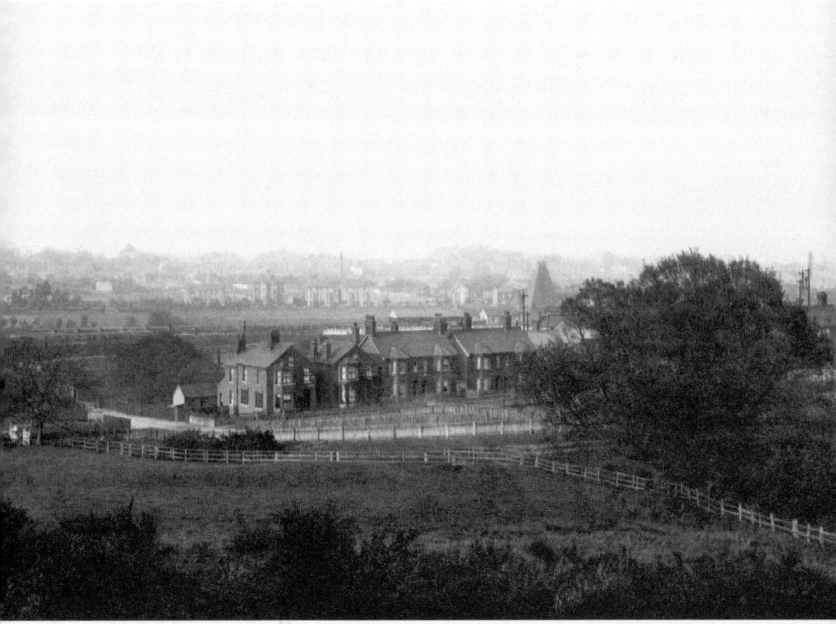

The railway arrived in Ipswich in 1846, and very quickly had an impact on industry and commerce. In 1860, a new station was opened at the north end of the tunnel through Stoke Hill, which then enabled the railway to be continued to Bury St Edmunds and Norwich.

FROM STOKE HILL

1893 / 32198

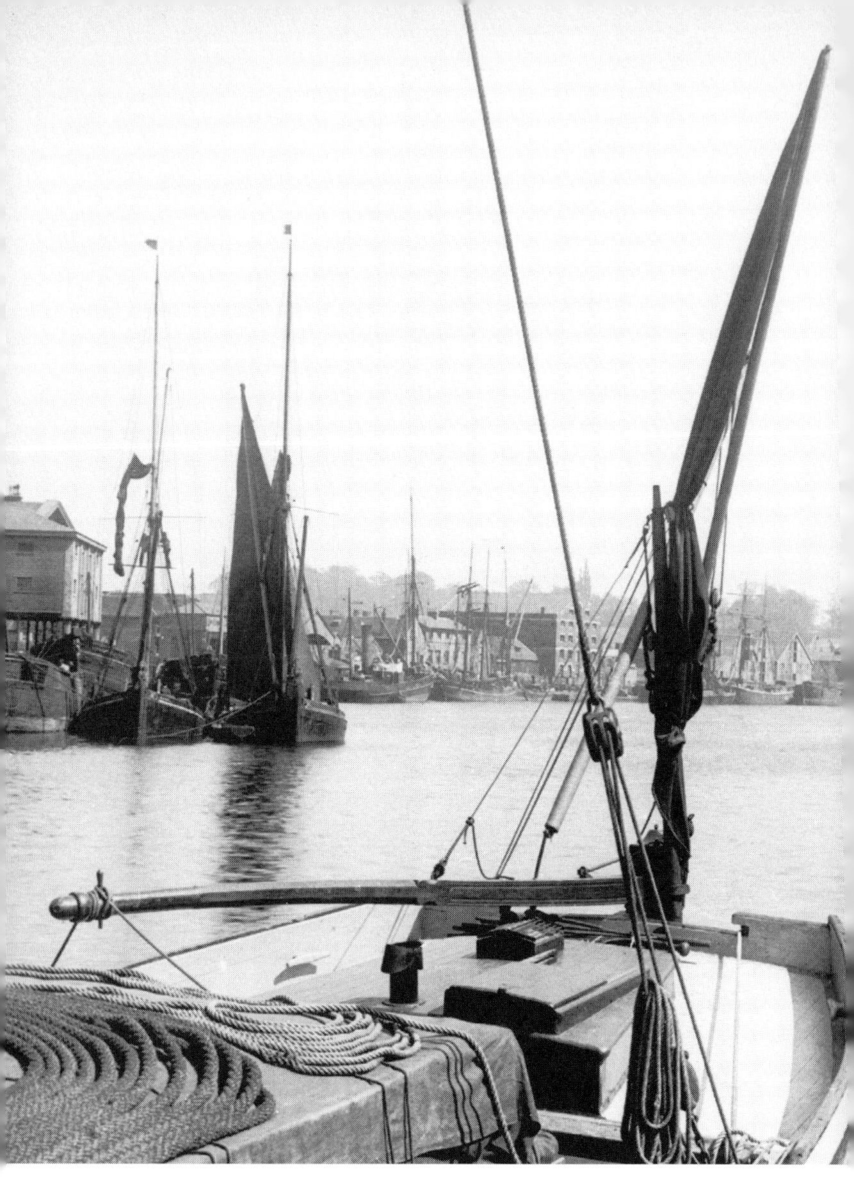

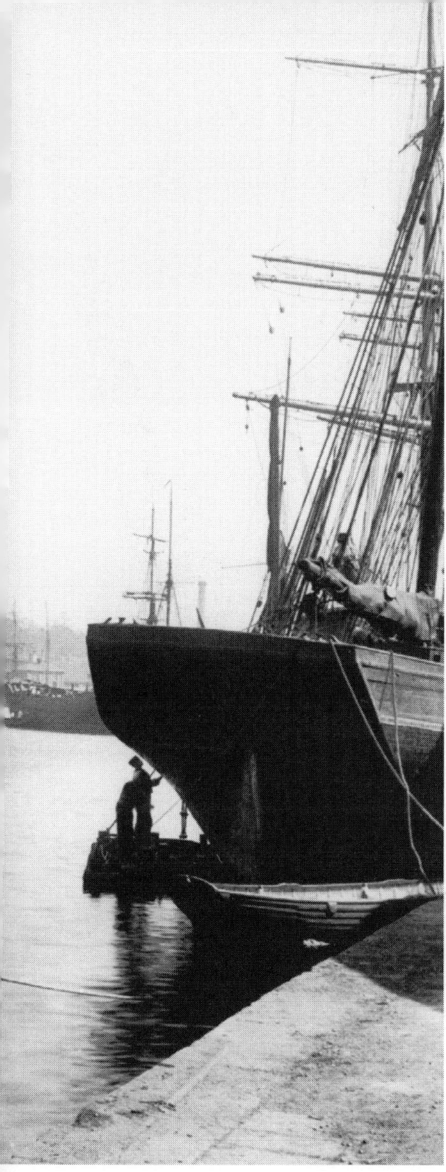

Ipswich, at the head of the Orwell Estuary, has been a major port for centuries. When this picture was taken, the port was starting to enjoy commercial success after a long period of decline.

THE DOCKS

1893 / 32208

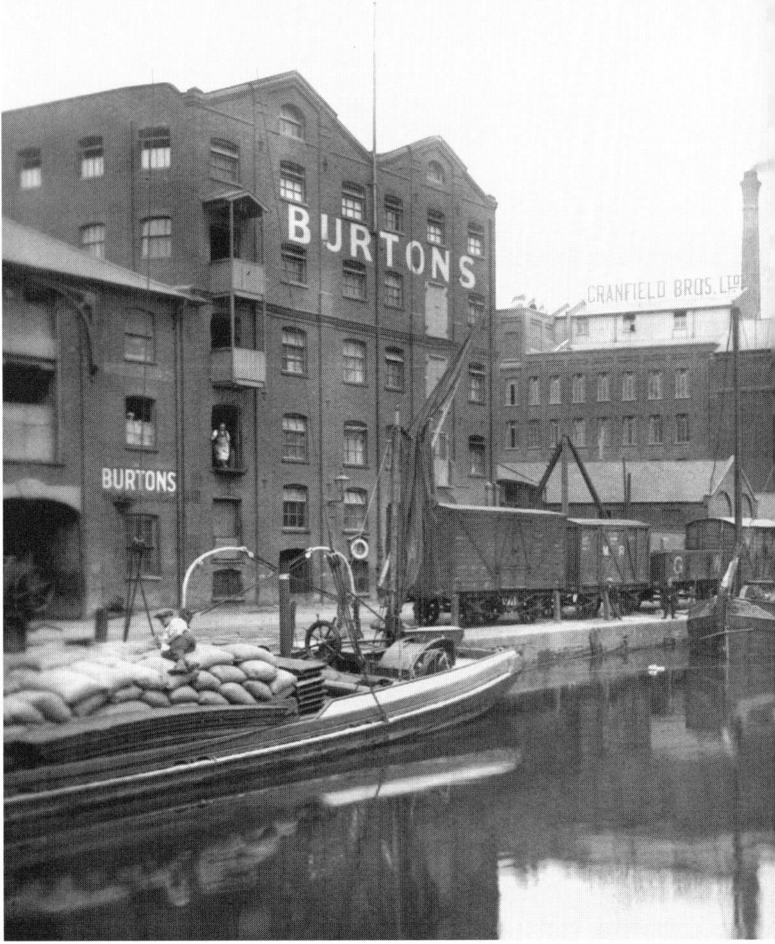

ST PETER'S DOCK

1921 / 70411

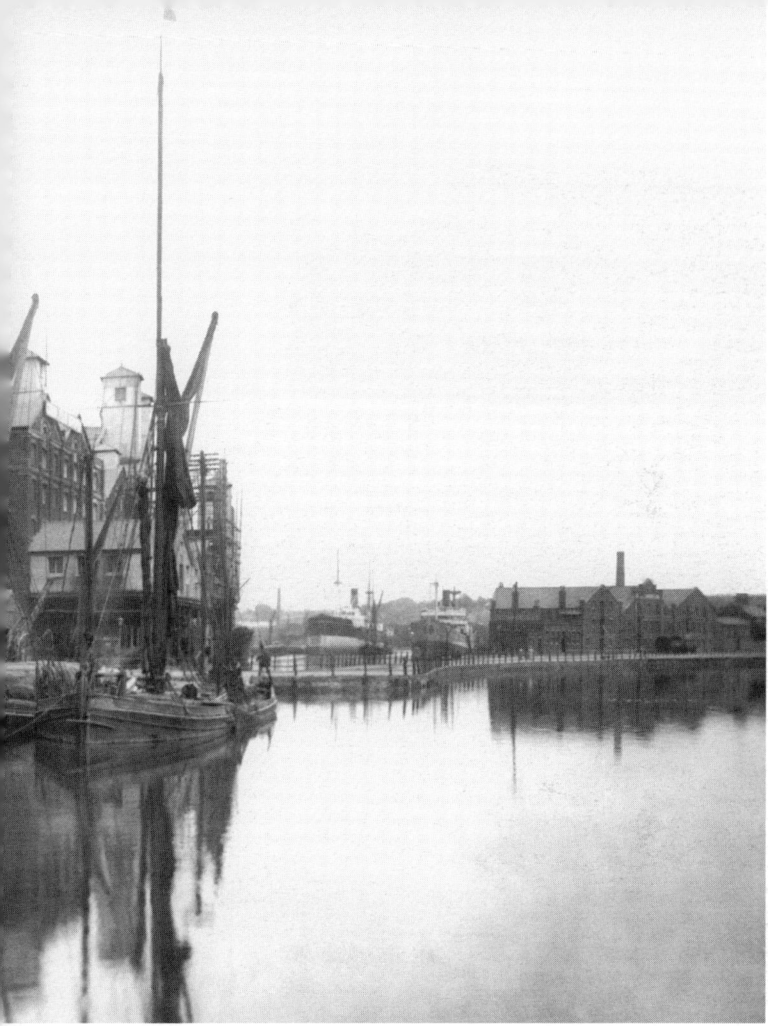

Sailing barges are tied up in the Wet Dock, the non-tidal part of the port of Ipswich. Adjacent to the dock are large warehouses, including that of Cranfields, who along with Pauls owned their own large fleets of barges.

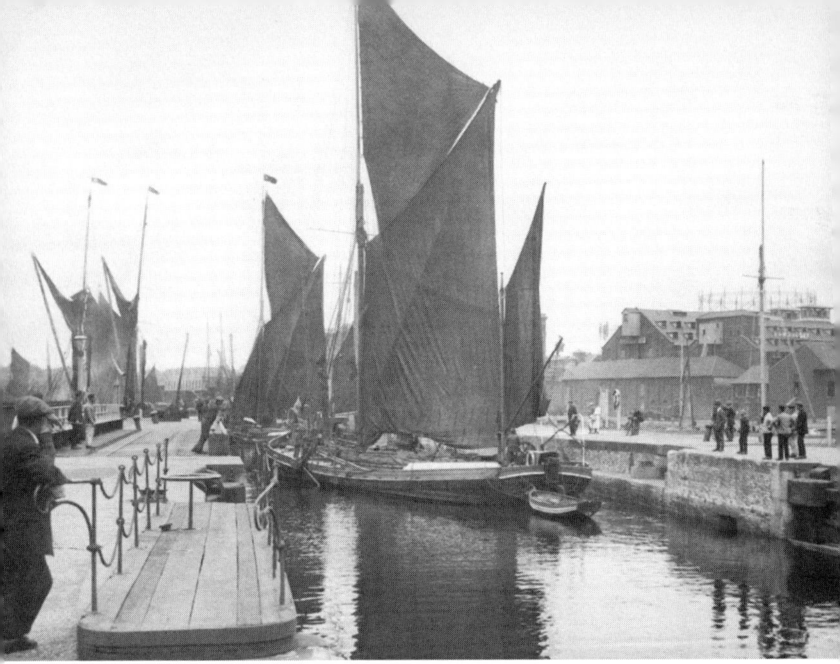

A sailing barge negotiates the lock gates. The Wet Dock was constructed between 1839 and 1842, and at the time it was the most revolutionary and the biggest of its kind in the country.

THE LOCK GATES

1921 / 70413

THE DOCK ENTRANCE

C1955 / I18050

What makes the Wet Dock so useful is that it is a non-tidal section of the port. Water in the dock is held at a constant level by the lock gates.

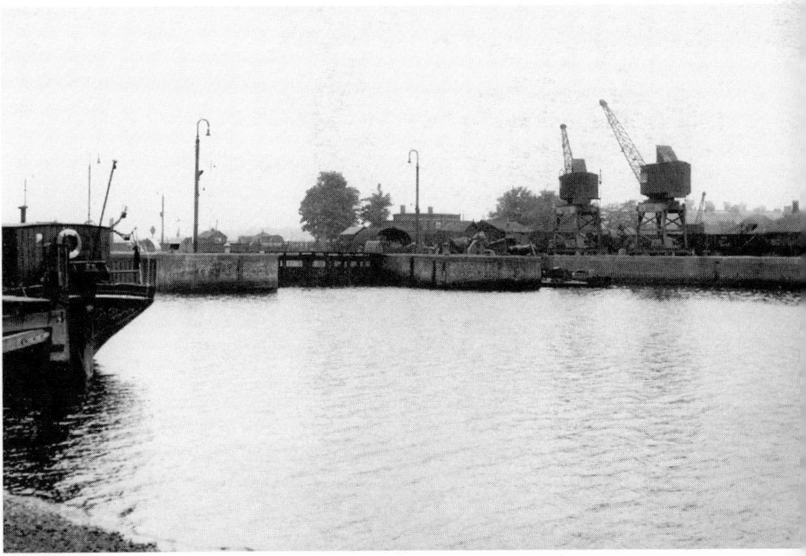

Sailing barges are moored on the river. Vessels like these were very much the mainstay of trade along the east coast, although by the time this photograph was taken, their days were certainly numbered.

THE DOCKS

1921 / 70412

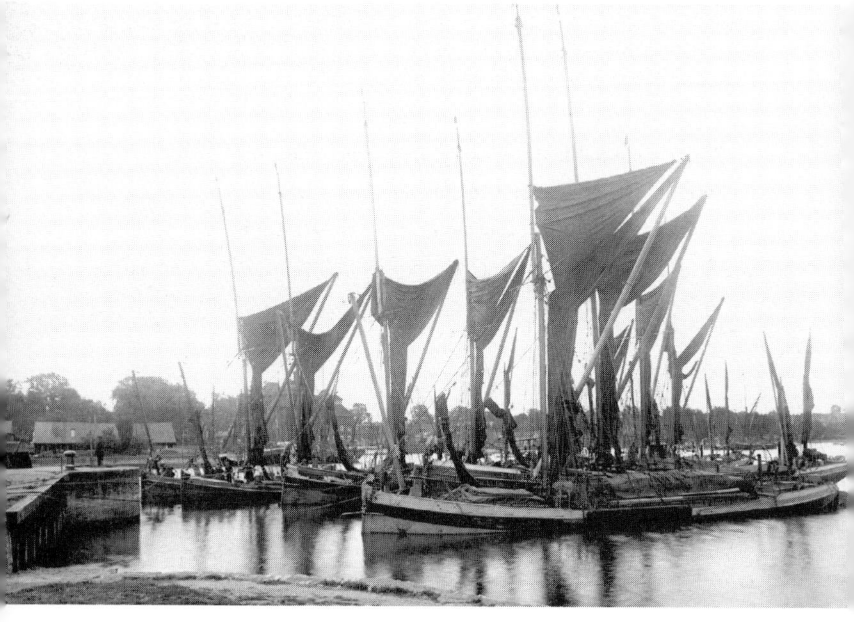

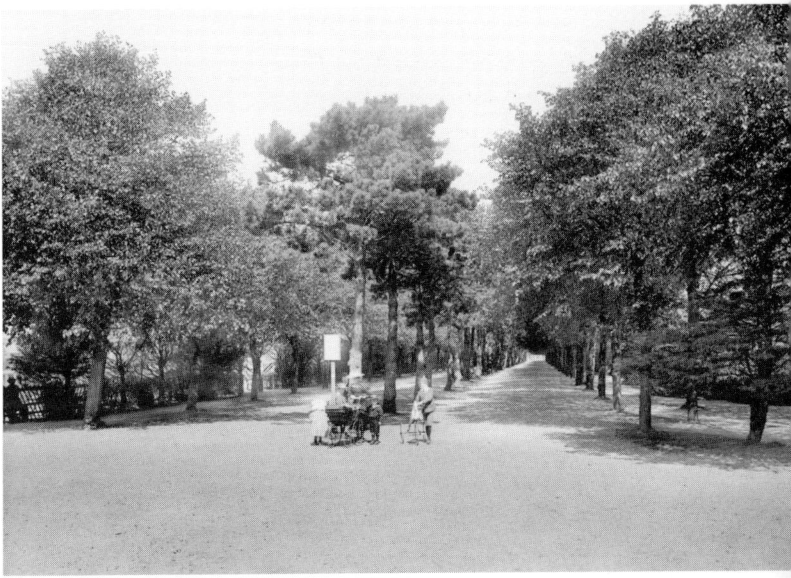

This is a somewhat staged family photograph. This tree-lined avenue, which ran alongside the New Cut - the channel taking vessels from the river to the Wet Dock - was a favourite walk for the townsfolk of Ipswich. It was lost to further development of the docks.

THE PROMENADE

1893 / 32210

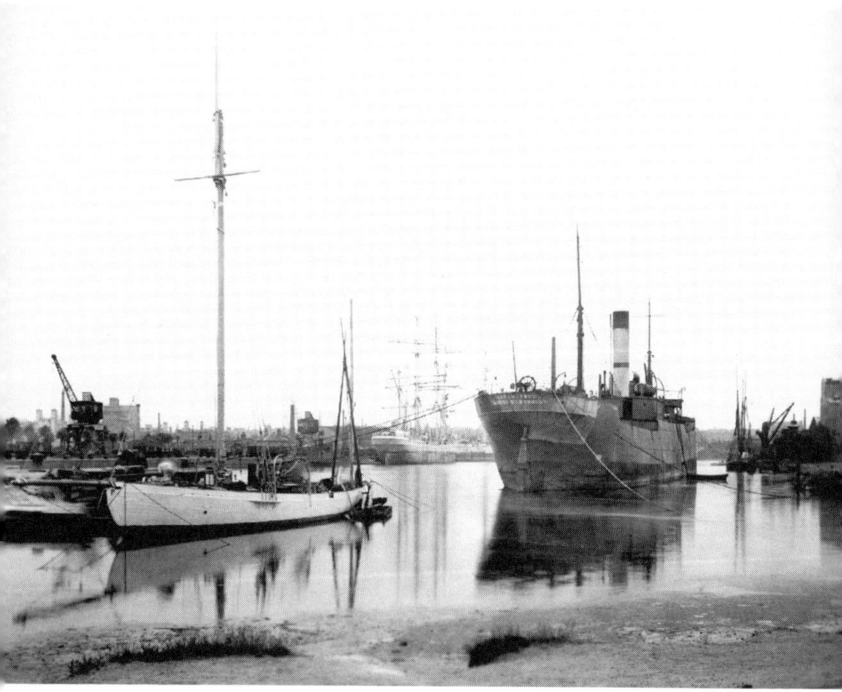

The old and new come together in this post-World War I photograph, with a steamer in the foreground, and a sailing ship in the distance.

THE DOCKS

1921 / 70415

A sailing barge makes its way along the Orwell, with lush wooded hillsides coming down to meet the broad tidal mudflats at the water's edge.

ON THE RIVER ORWELL

1909 / 61993

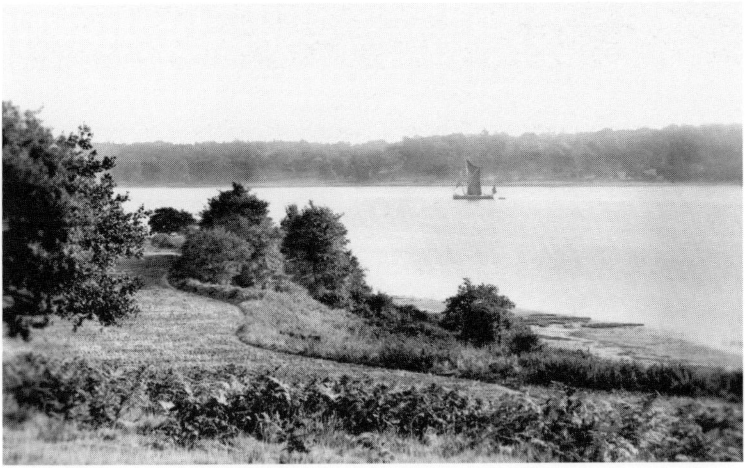

The name Hog Island has faded into history, although it lives on as a number of locations in New England.

HOG ISLAND

1921 / 70416

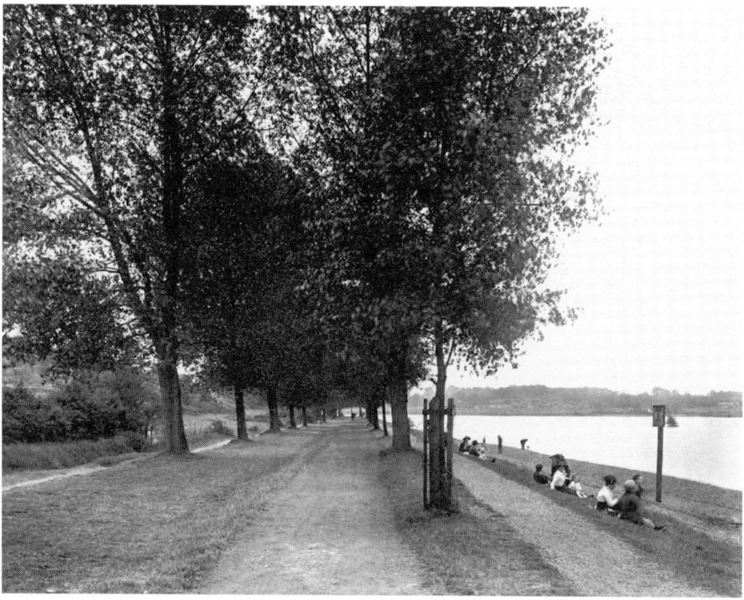

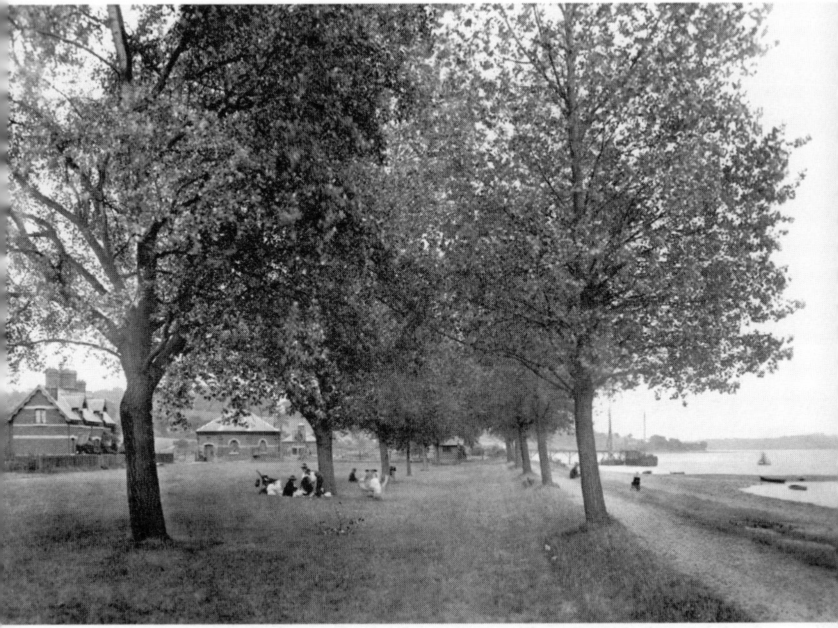

Once a popular riverside haunt for the locals, Hog Island is now known as Piper's Vale, and is more remarkable today as the north-eastern end of the Orwell Bridge.

HOG ISLAND

1921 / 70417

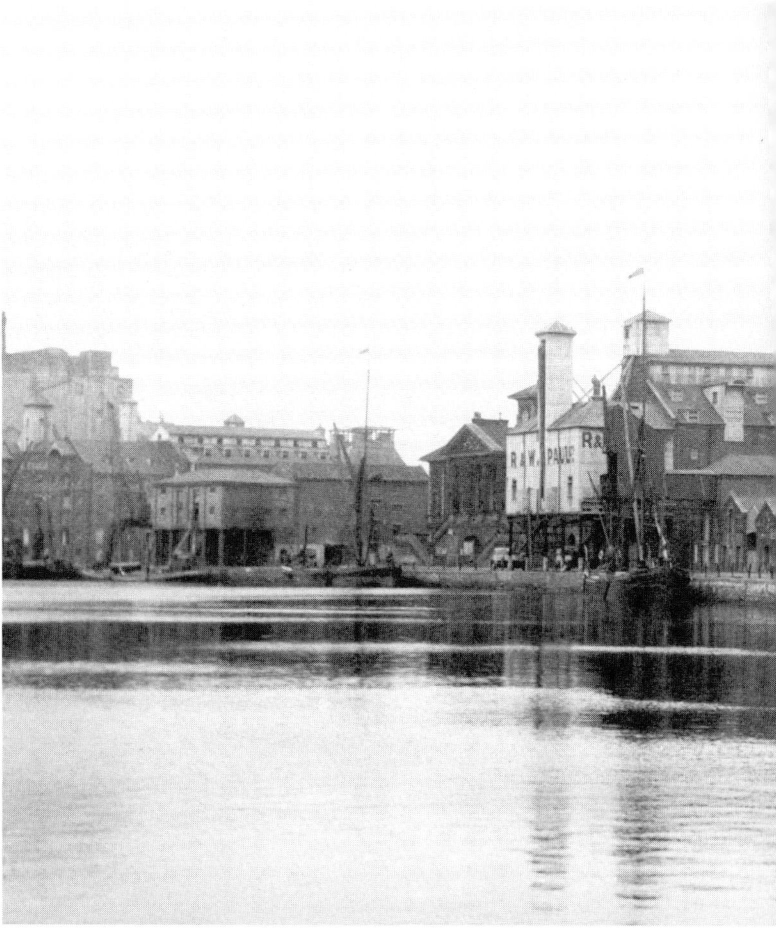

THE DOCKS

C1955 / I18049

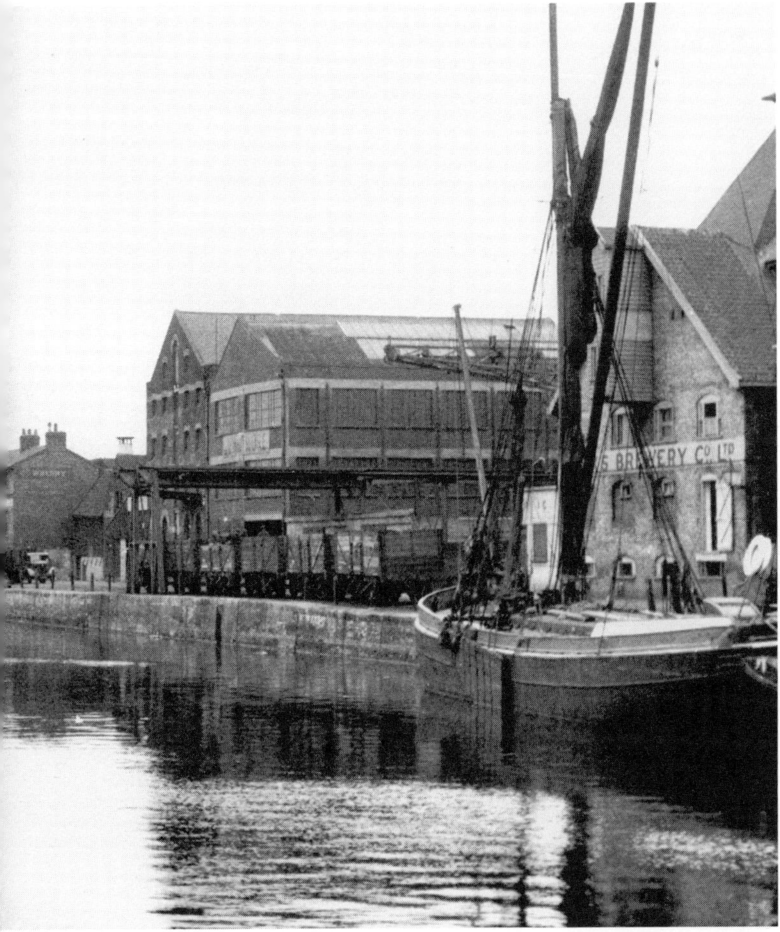

East Anglia has a long tradition for growing malting barley, and Ipswich had a number of maltings. R & W Paul's was right on the dockside.

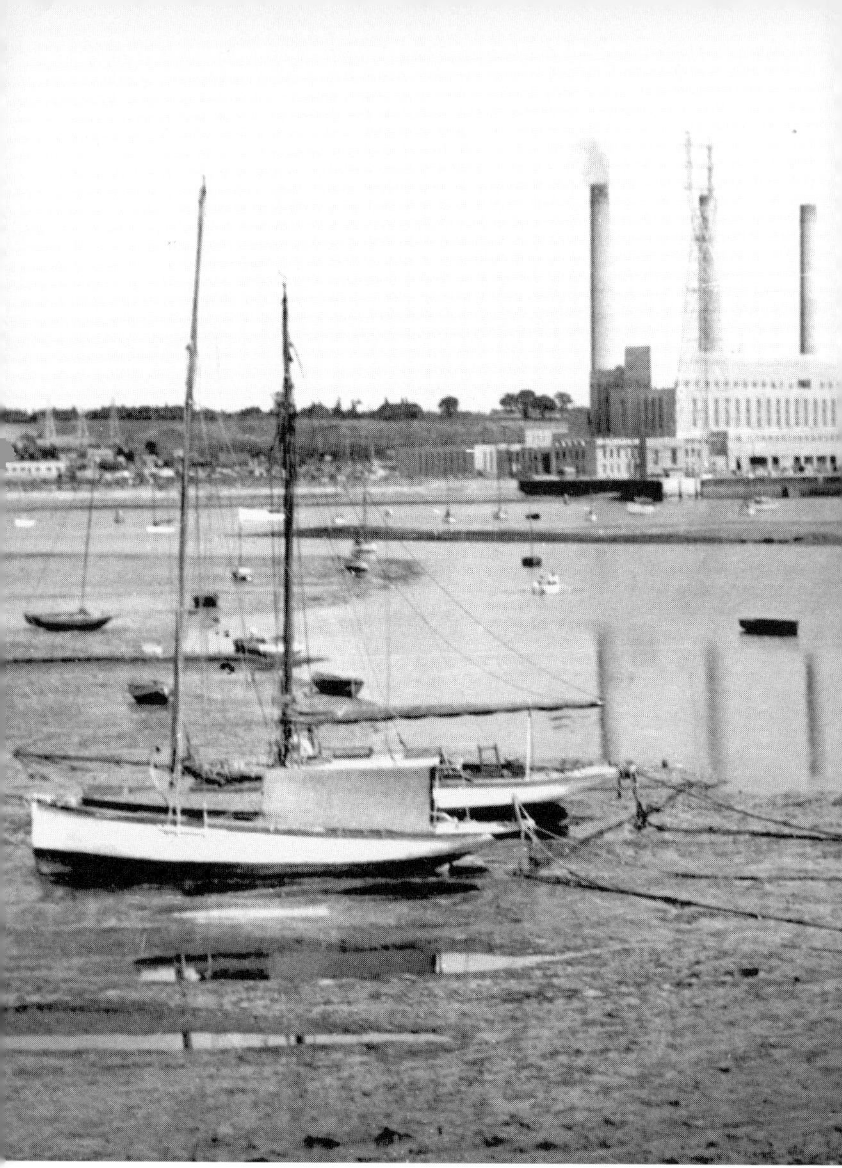

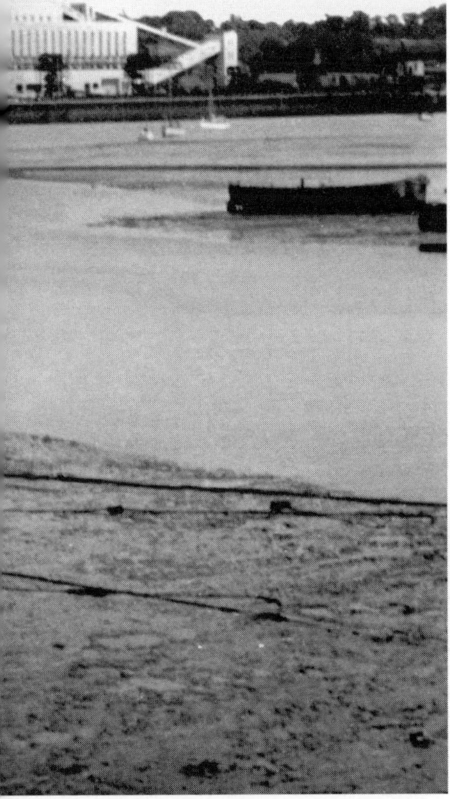

A 20th-century means of producing power shares the banks of the Orwell with vessels which harness one of the oldest forms of power. With shallow mudflats along the banks of the tidal Orwell estuary, moored sailing boats end up on their keels twice a day.

THE POWER STATION

C1955 / I18020

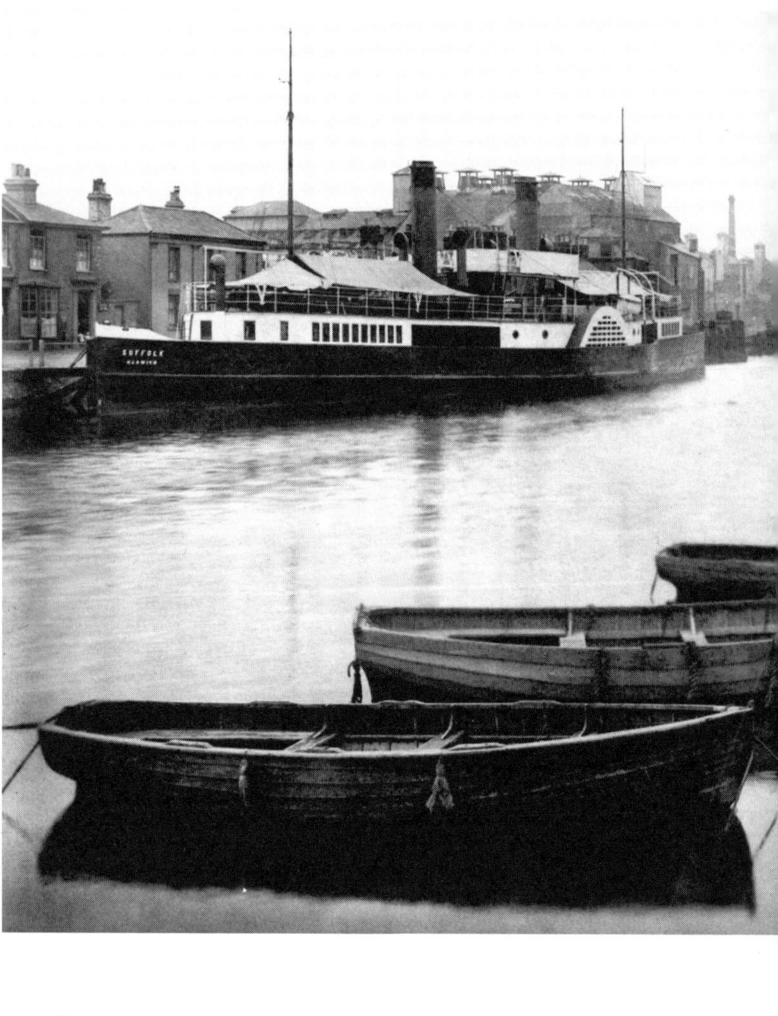

THE RIVER ORWELL
IPSWICH STEAM BOATS

1921 / 70410

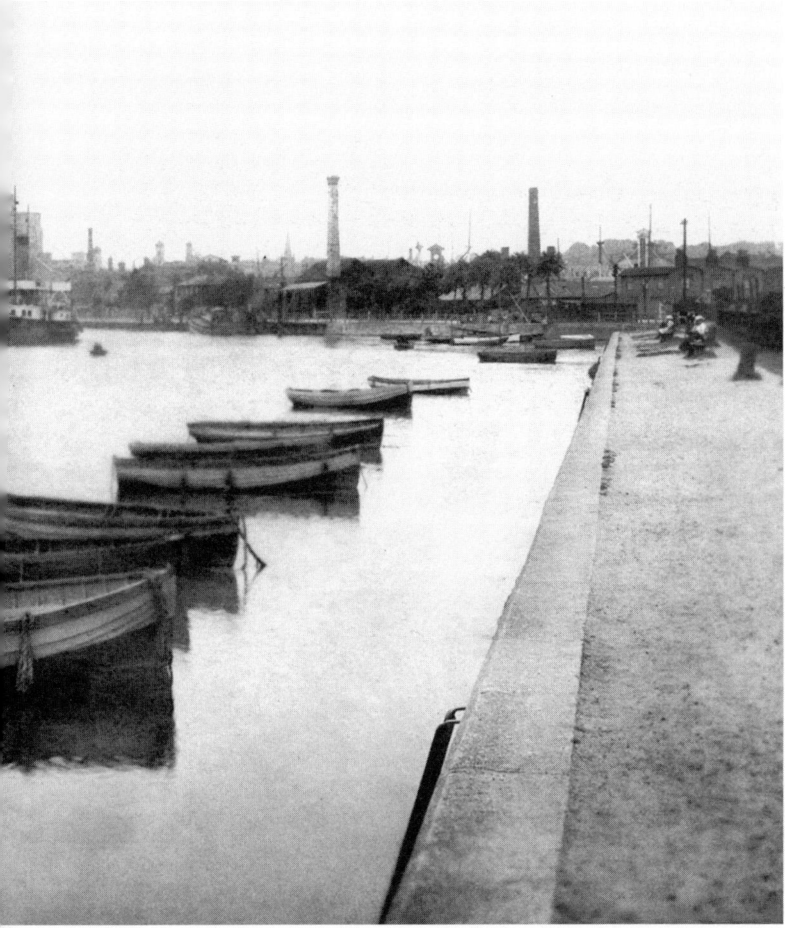

Paddle steamers provided pleasure trips and a bus service of sorts out to the coastal ports of Harwich and Felixstowe. Peering above the SS Suffolk are the tell-tale signs of Ipswich's malting industry.

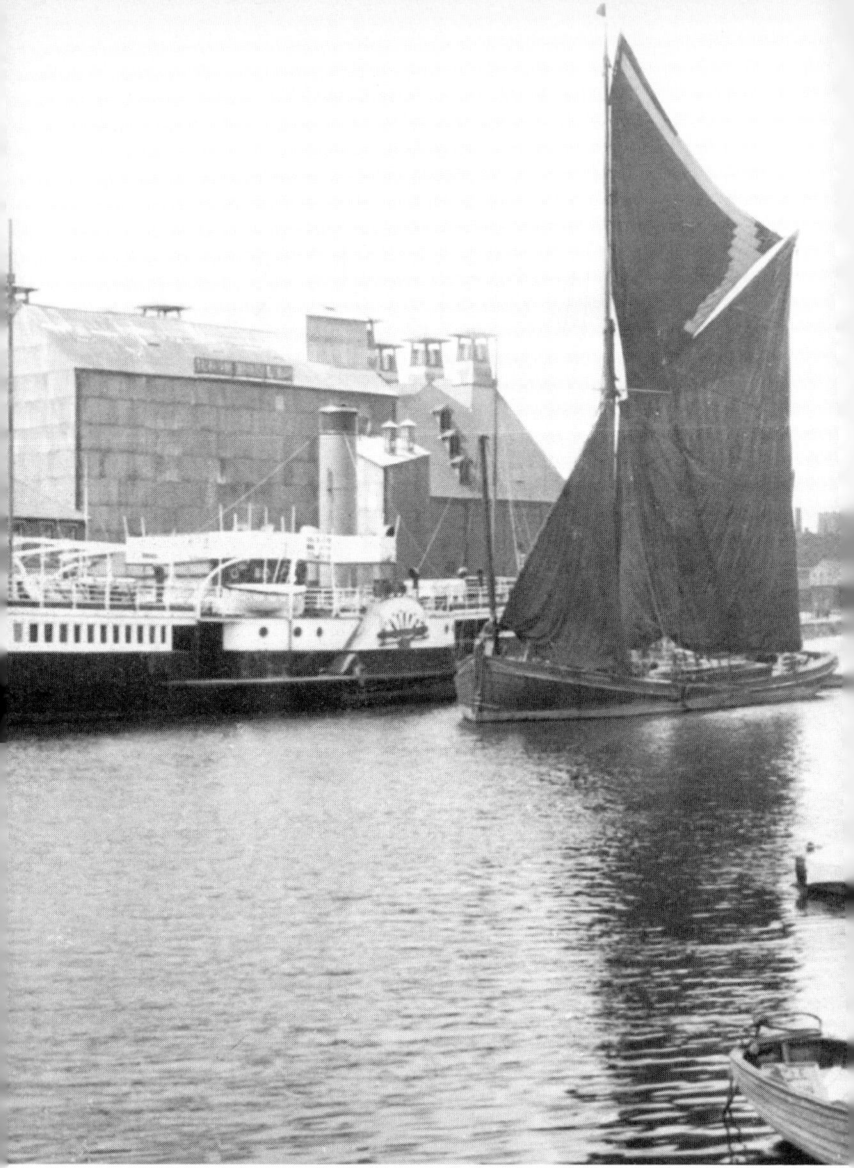

THE RIVER ORWELL

1921 / 70414

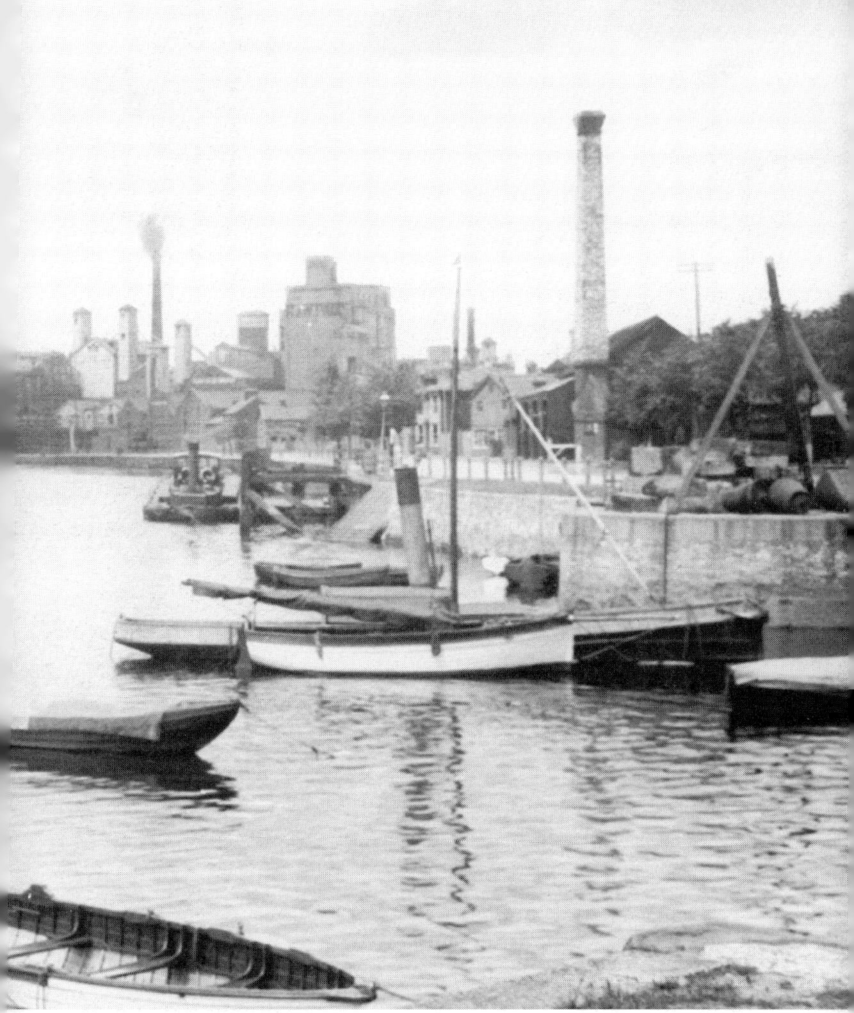

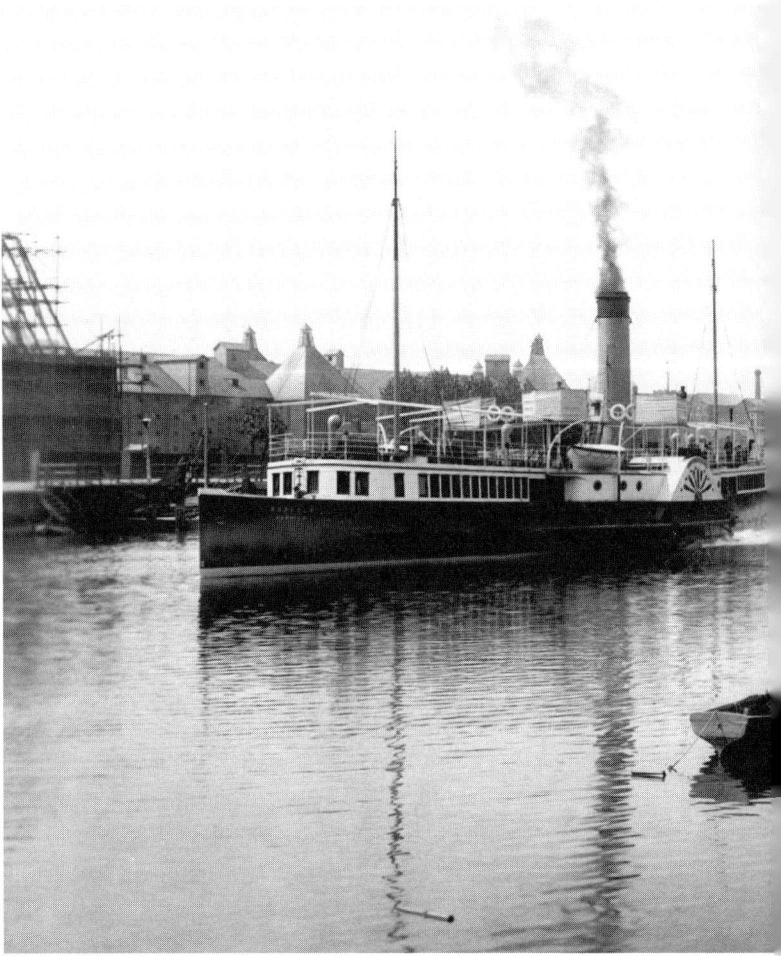

THE RIVER ORWELL
AND SS 'NORFOLK'

1904 / 51246

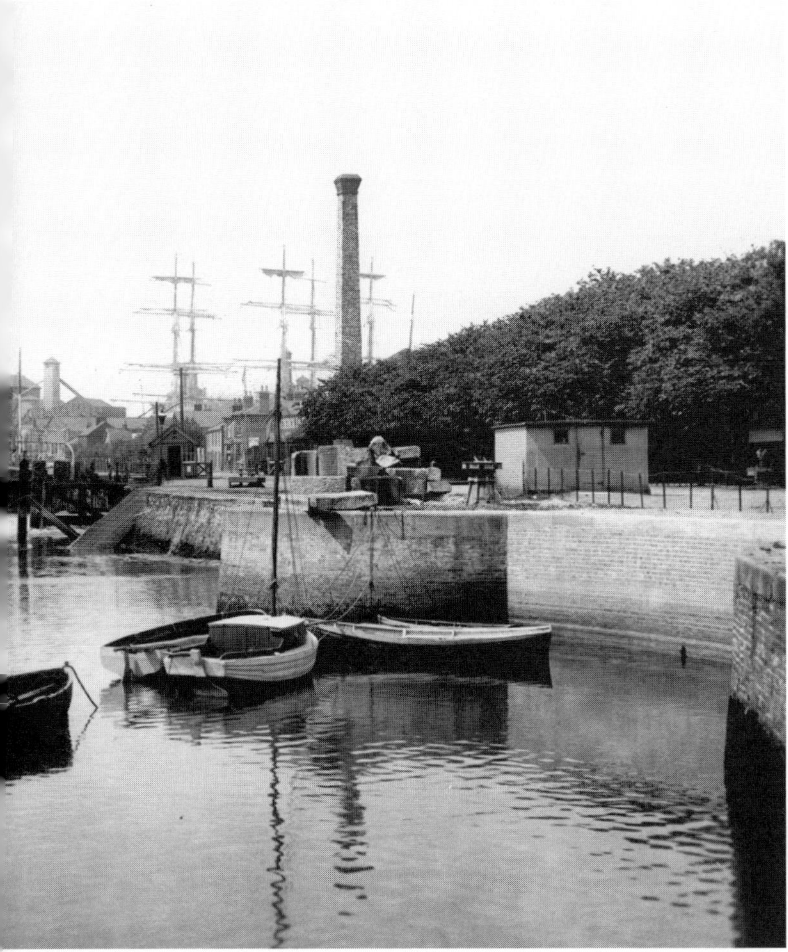

Paddle steamers like this one used to operate along the East Coast, running pleasure trips to places like Felixstowe and Harwich. In the background are the masts of cargo ships.

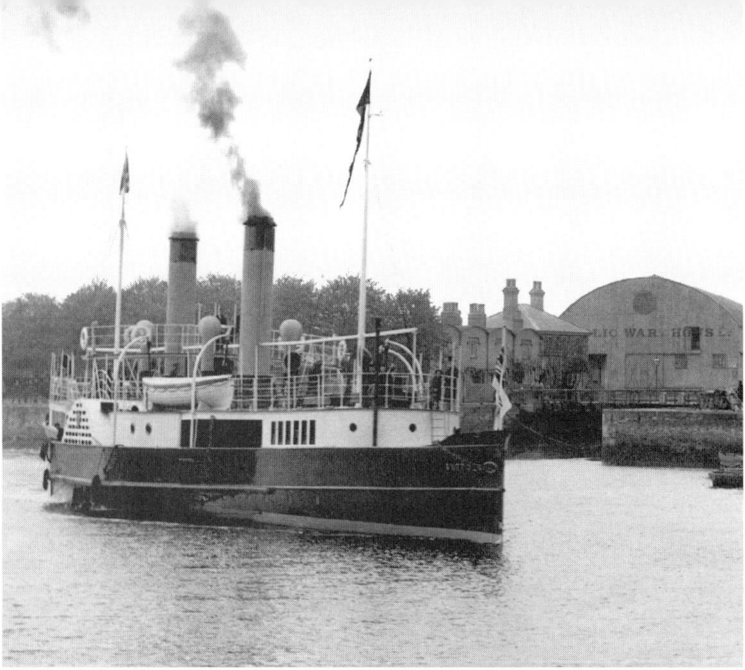

Looking at the lifeboat hanging from the davits (presumably there was one on the other side), one is tempted to wonder whether they would have been sufficient to cope in an emergency if this paddle steamer was fully laden. Up until the inquiry which followed the 'Titanic' disaster in 1912, lifeboat capacity on steamers was based on the ship's tonnage rather than the actual number of people carried.

SS 'SUFFOLK'

1896 / 37315

ON THE GIPPING

1894 / 34817

Upstream from the docks, the river which flows through Ipswich is called the Gipping (hence the Saxon origins of the town's name - Gippeswic). Clearly, the prospects for rowing here look good.

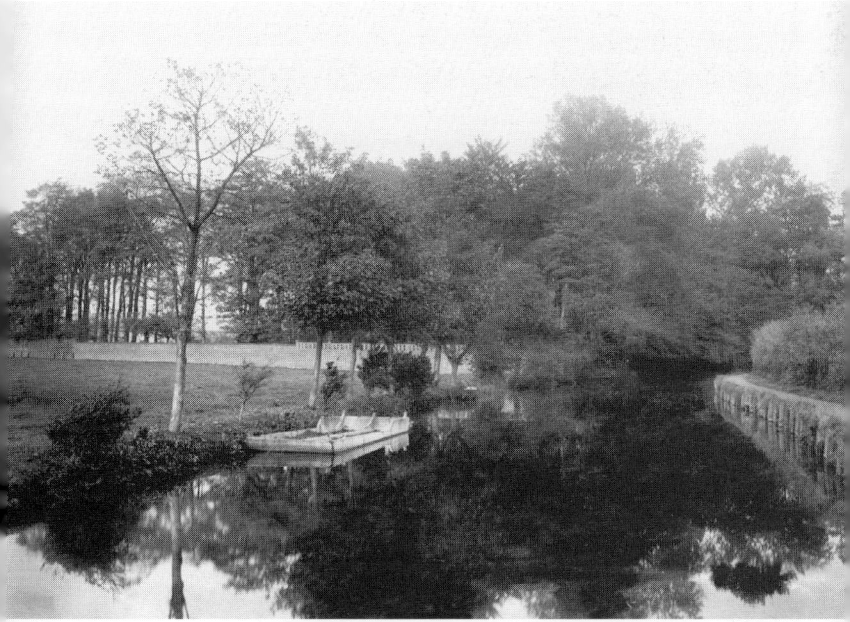

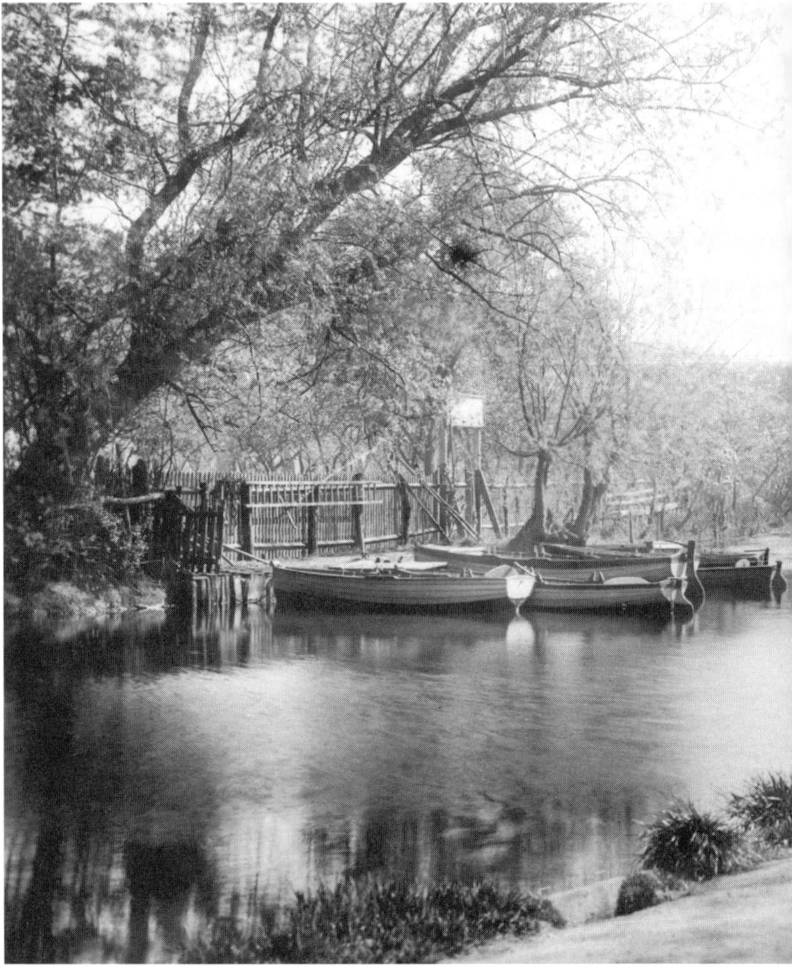

ON THE GIPPING

1893 / 32209

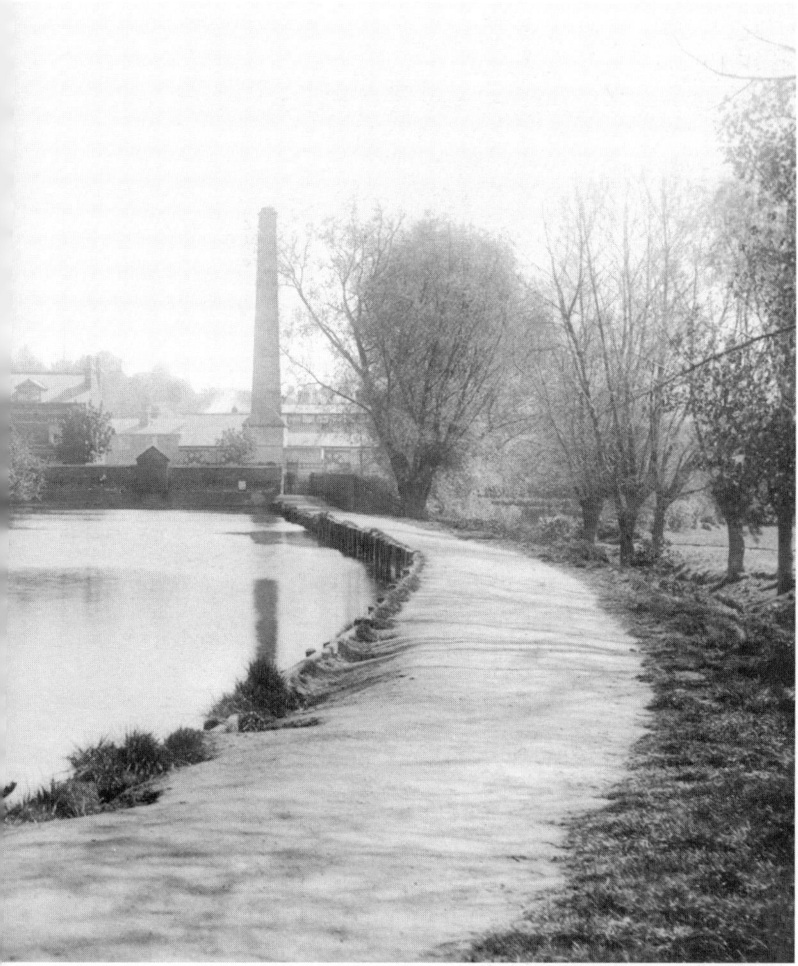

This is a picture of tranquillity perhaps, but the Gipping was effectively a canal with a tow path, made to assist the carriage of goods upstream as far as Stowmarket.

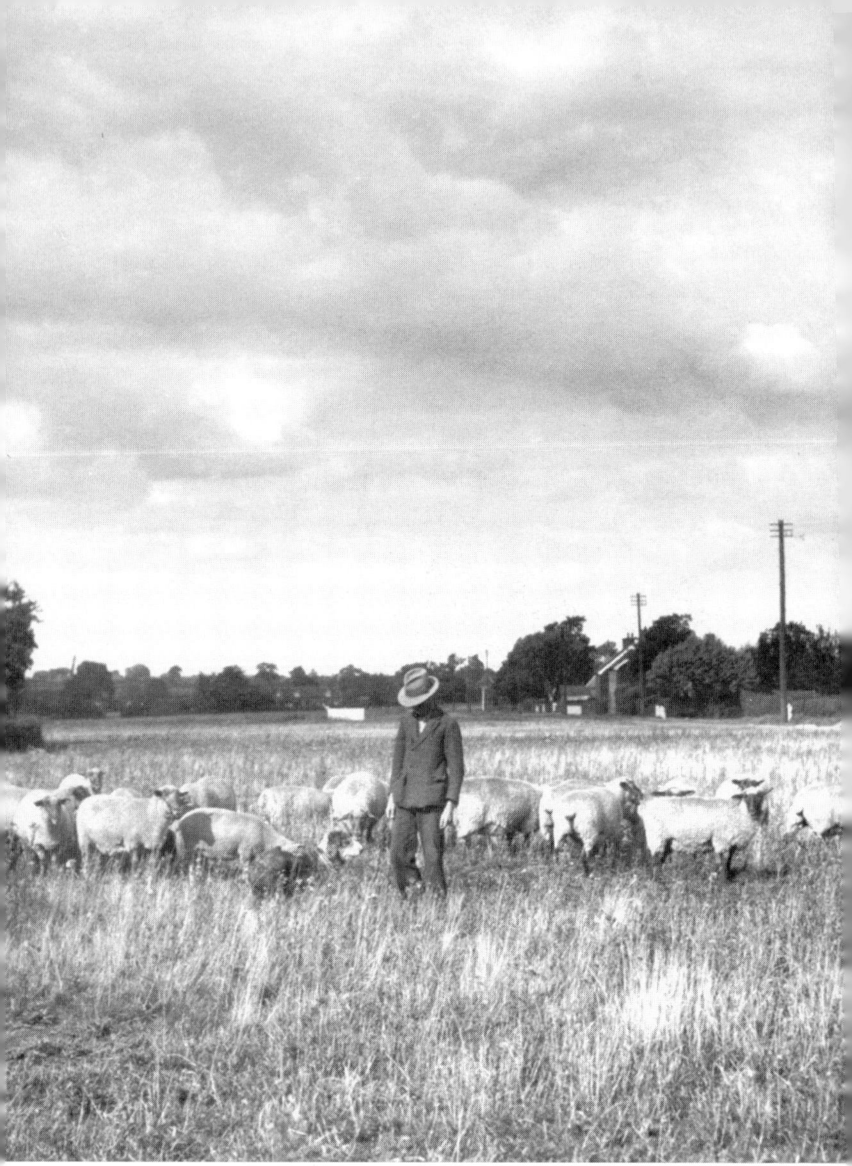

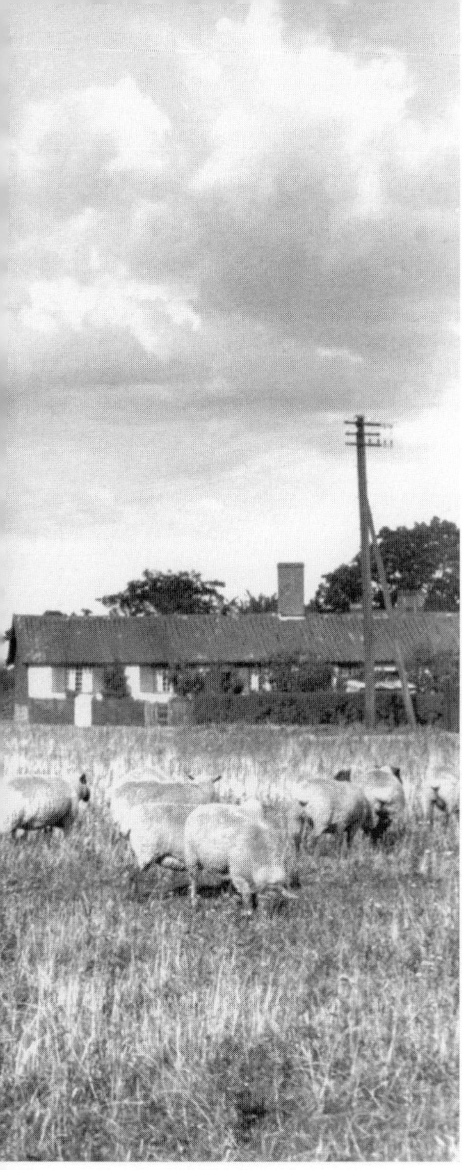

A between-the-wars picture of pastoral tranquillity. The only slightly odd element of the photograph is the shepherd himself - the suit and hat do not quite fit the stereotyped image!

BARKING TYE
THE SHEPHERD

1934 / 86420

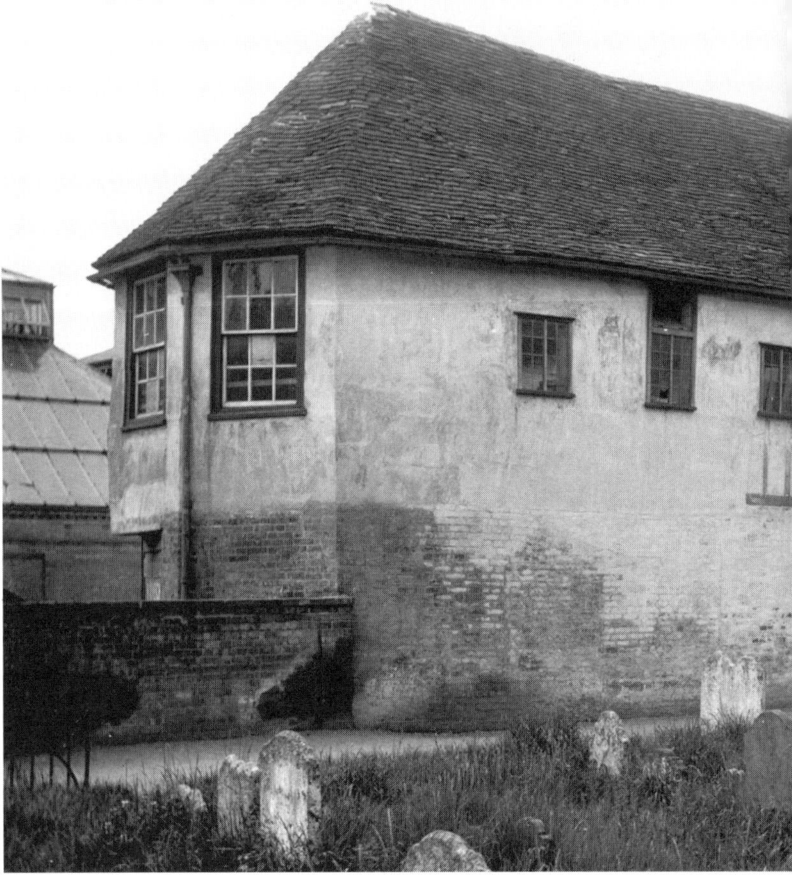

HADLEIGH, THE GUILDHALL

1922 / 71975

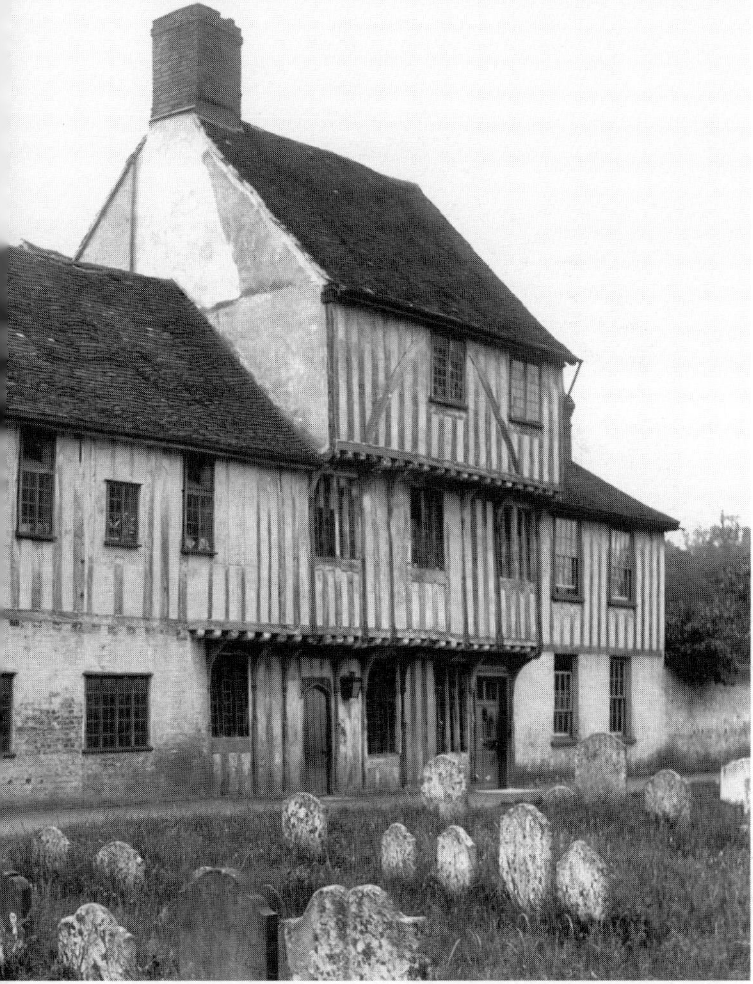

Timbers this close together were not required for structural integrity: rather, they were a sign of opulence. Hadleigh's 15th-century Guildhall, with its two overhanging upper storeys, remains as a reminder of the huge wealth generated by the medieval wool trade.

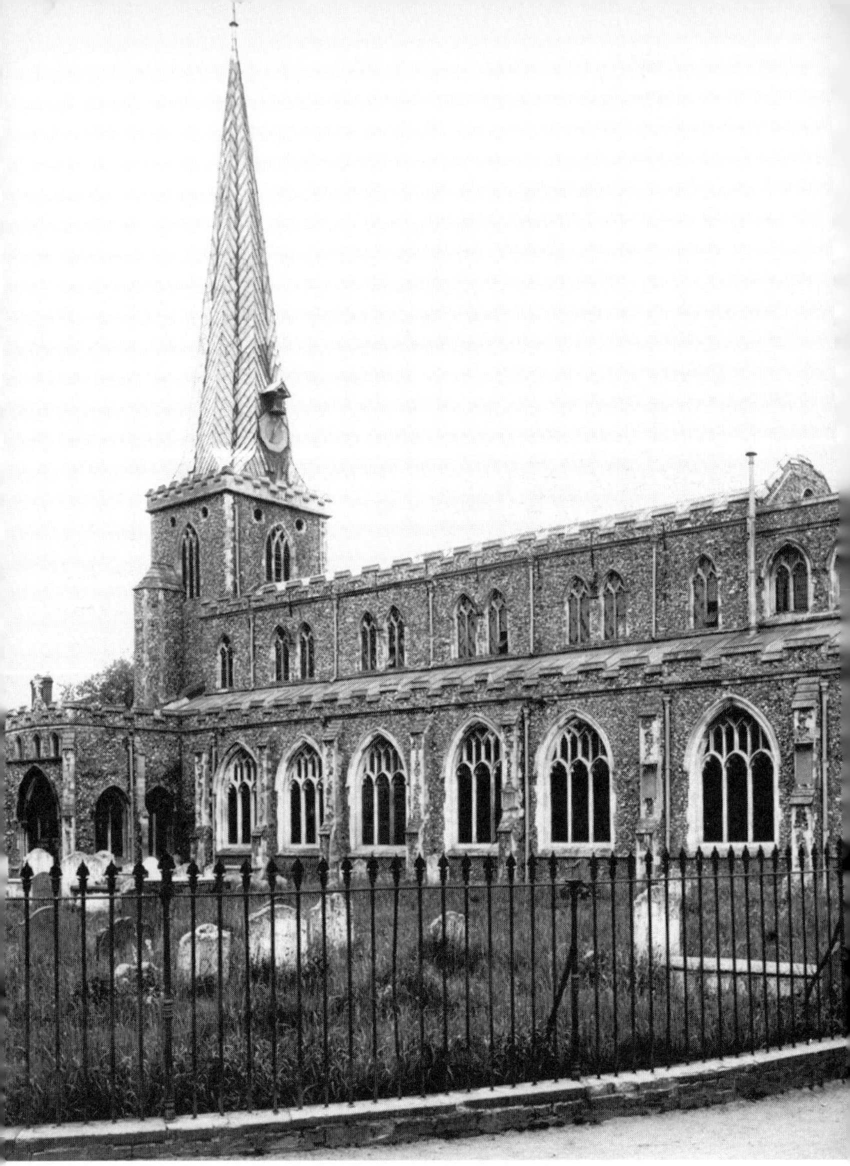

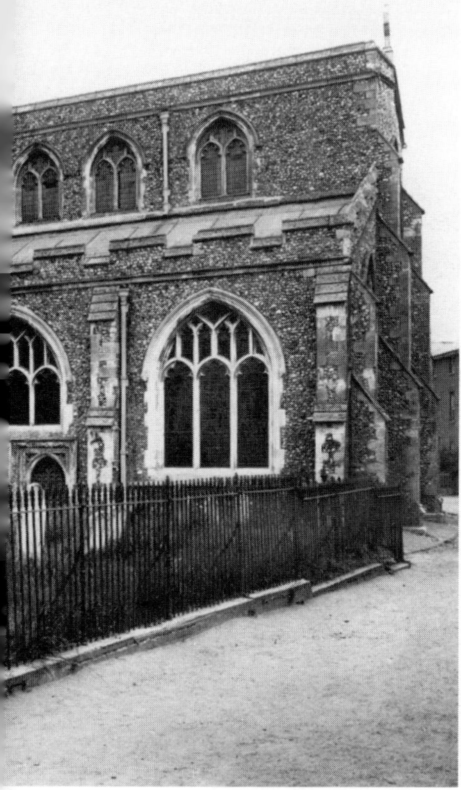

St Mary's, one of the largest in Suffolk, is not a typical Suffolk wool church, and has an elegant lead spire. Inside is the 600-year-old Angelus Bell, one of the oldest in the country, which is inscribed 'Ave Maria Gracia Plena Dominus Tecum'. Perhaps the man who made the bell had other things on his mind when it came to putting in the inscription, as he forgot to invert the words laterally in the mould, and they appear backwards on the finished article!

HADLEIGH
ST MARY'S
CHURCH

1922 / 71972

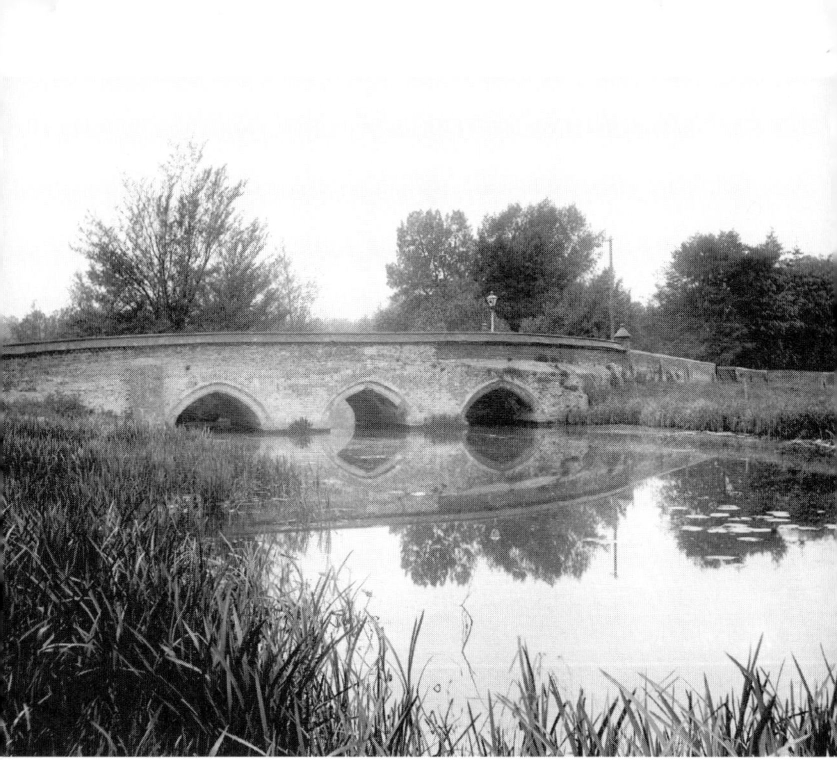

This is the three-arched red brick medieval bridge over the River Brett at Hadleigh. King Guthrum, the first Danish king of East Anglia, had a palace at Hadleigh, and it is reputed that he is buried in the church.

HADLEIGH, TOPPESFIELD BRIDGE

1922 / 71979

These are 17th-century buildings. The Coffee Tavern came into being around thirty years previously - it was an attempt to provide people with an alternative to nearby public houses.

HADLEIGH
OLD HOUSES IN THE HIGH STREET

1922 / 71970

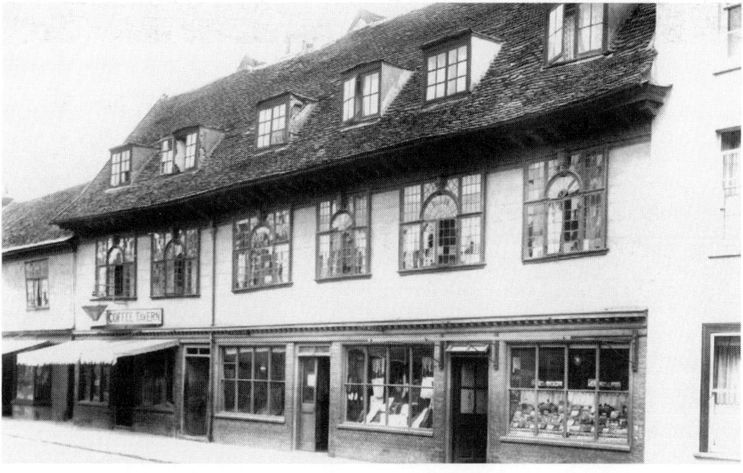

Shotley Gate, at the very end of the Shotley Peninsula, was home to the former HMS 'Ganges', the Royal Navy's training school. This shore establishment gave its young recruits a stiff taste of discipline to fit them for their careers in the Navy. Each boy would be required to climb the 150ft high mast from HMS 'Cordelia', and every year, cadets at the passing-out ceremony had to climb the rigging, the pride of place going to the 'button boy', who perched on the eleven-inch diameter top of the mast.

SHOTLEY GATE
THE VILLAGE

C1955 / S581011

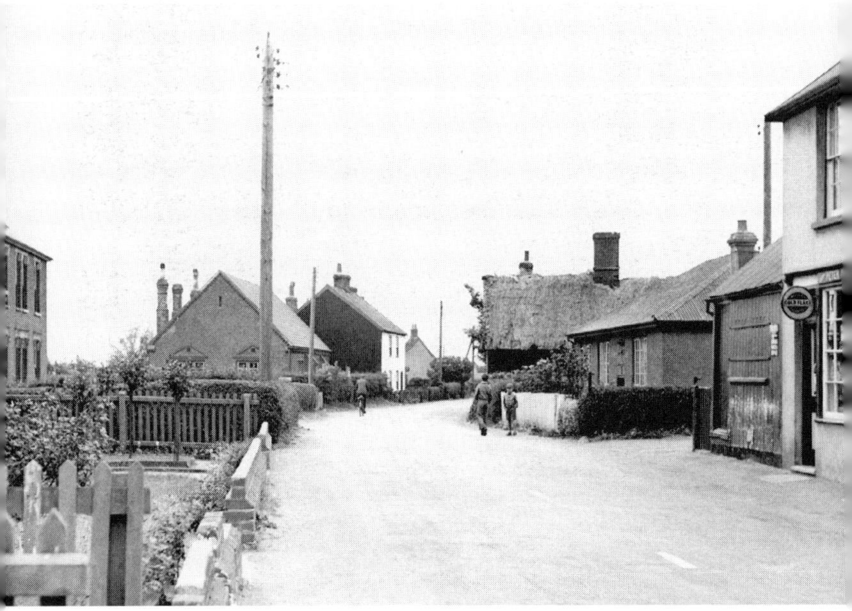

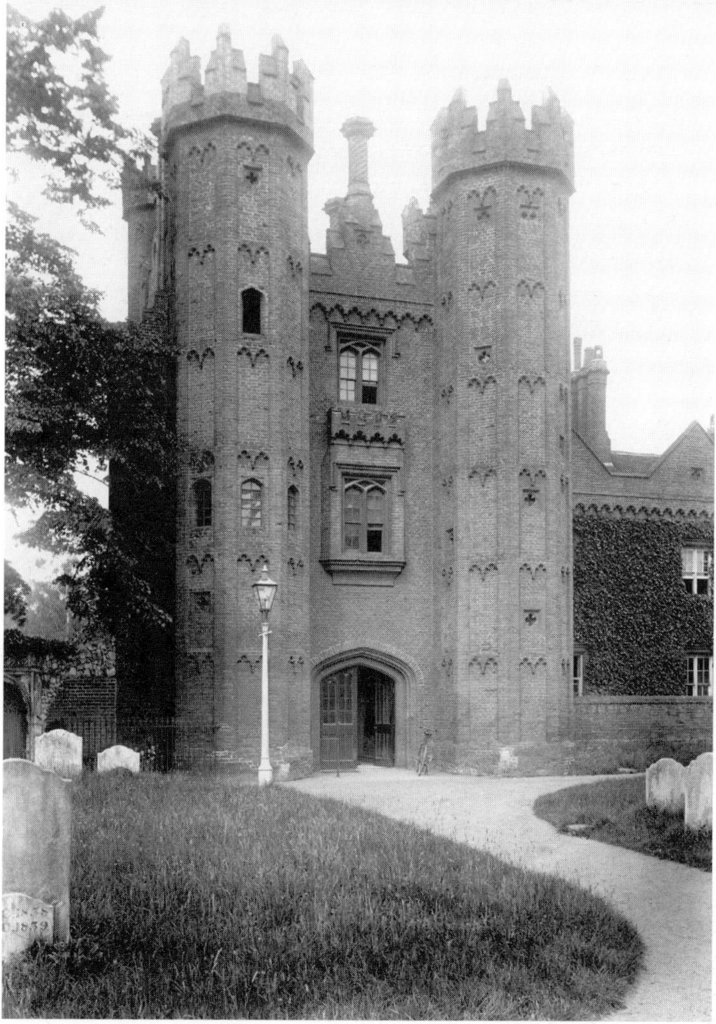

HADLEIGH
THE DEANERY TOWER

1922 / 71976

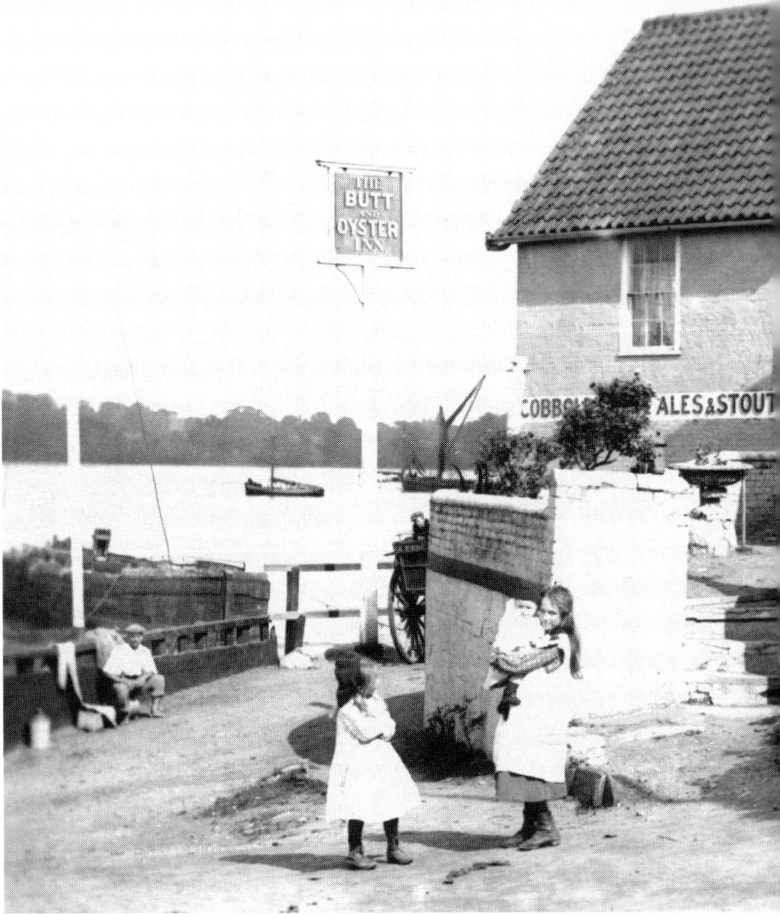

PIN MILL
THE BUTT AND OYSTER
1909 / 62001

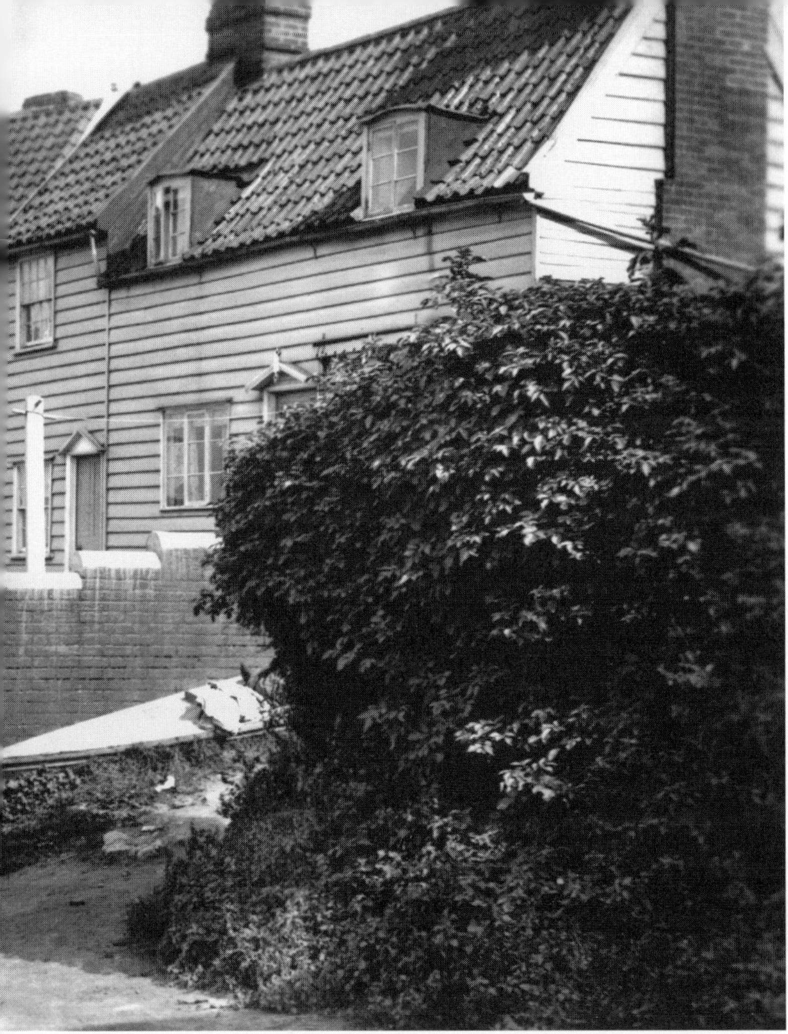

The Butt and Oyster is probably the most well-known pub on the East Coast, at Pin Mill, on the River Orwell. Across the river from here is Orwell Park, in the 18th century the home of 'Old Grog' - Admiral Vernon. It was he who won sailors their daily ration of grog - rum and water.

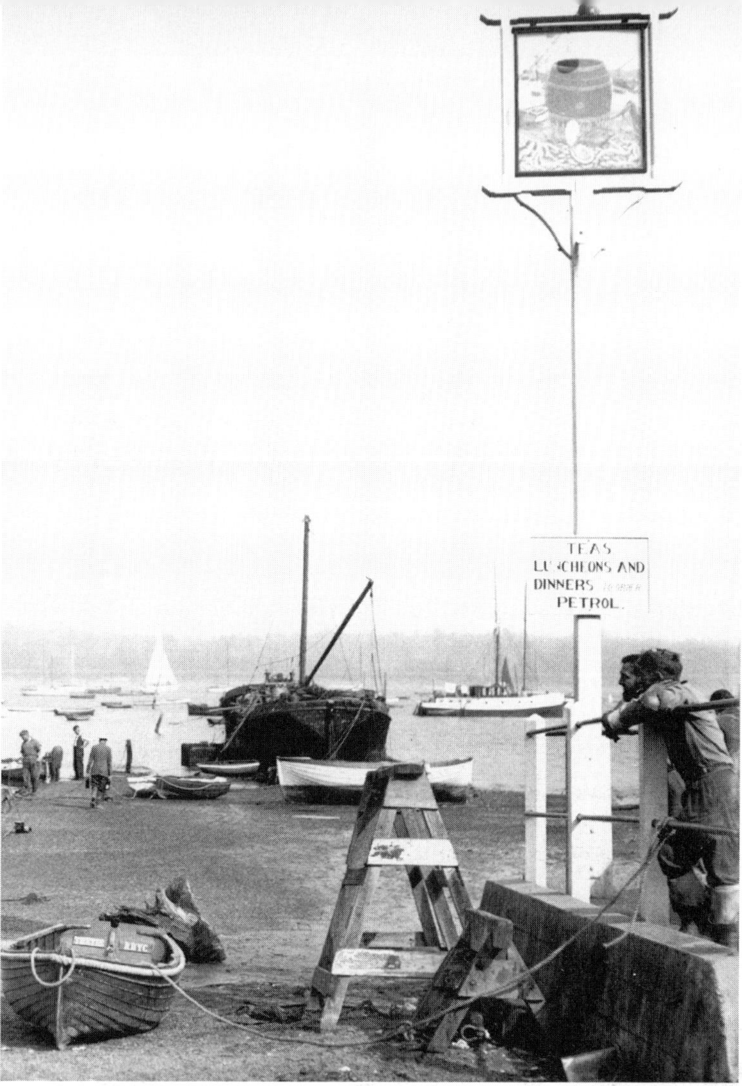

PIN MILL

c1960 / P370027

A sailing boat on the River Orwell - the pub here has long been a favourite with the yachting fraternity.

PIN MILL
THE RIVER

1909 / 61998

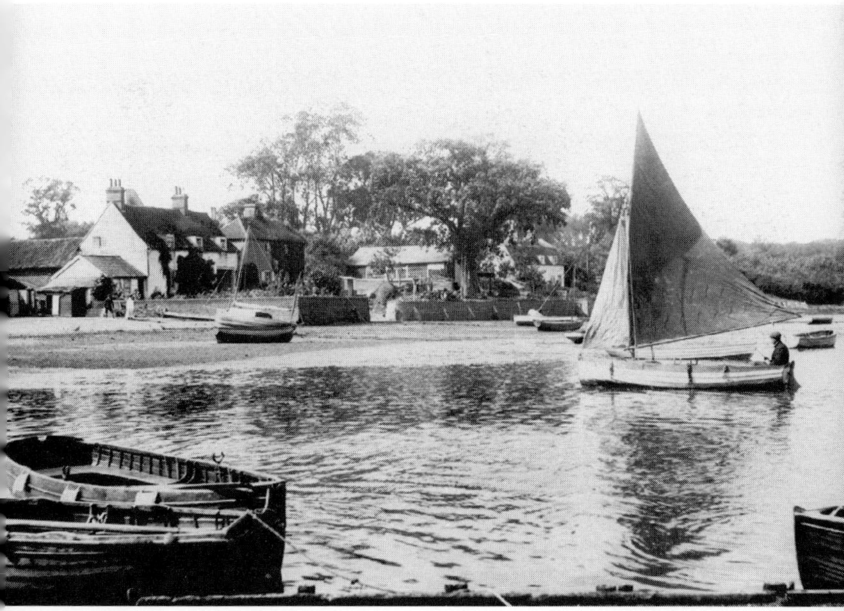

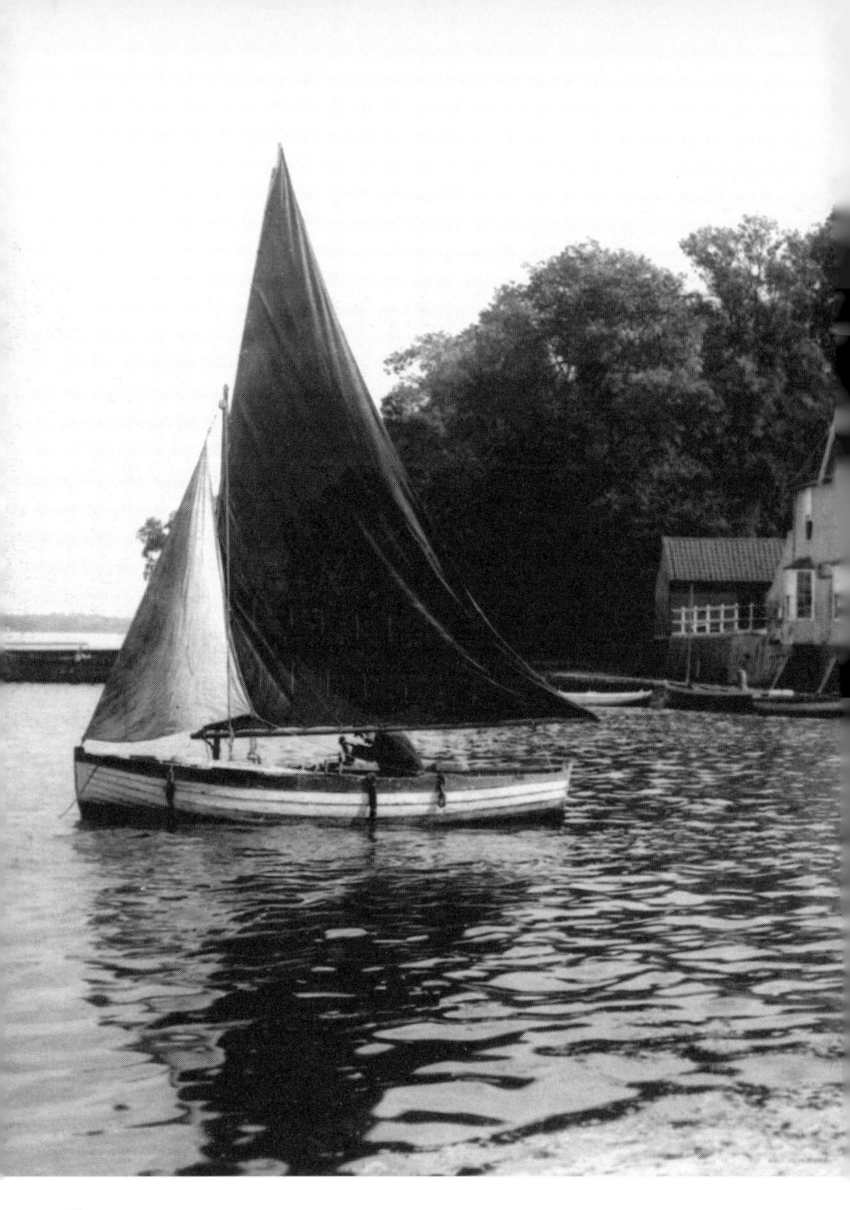

PIN MILL, WATERSIDE

1909 / 62000

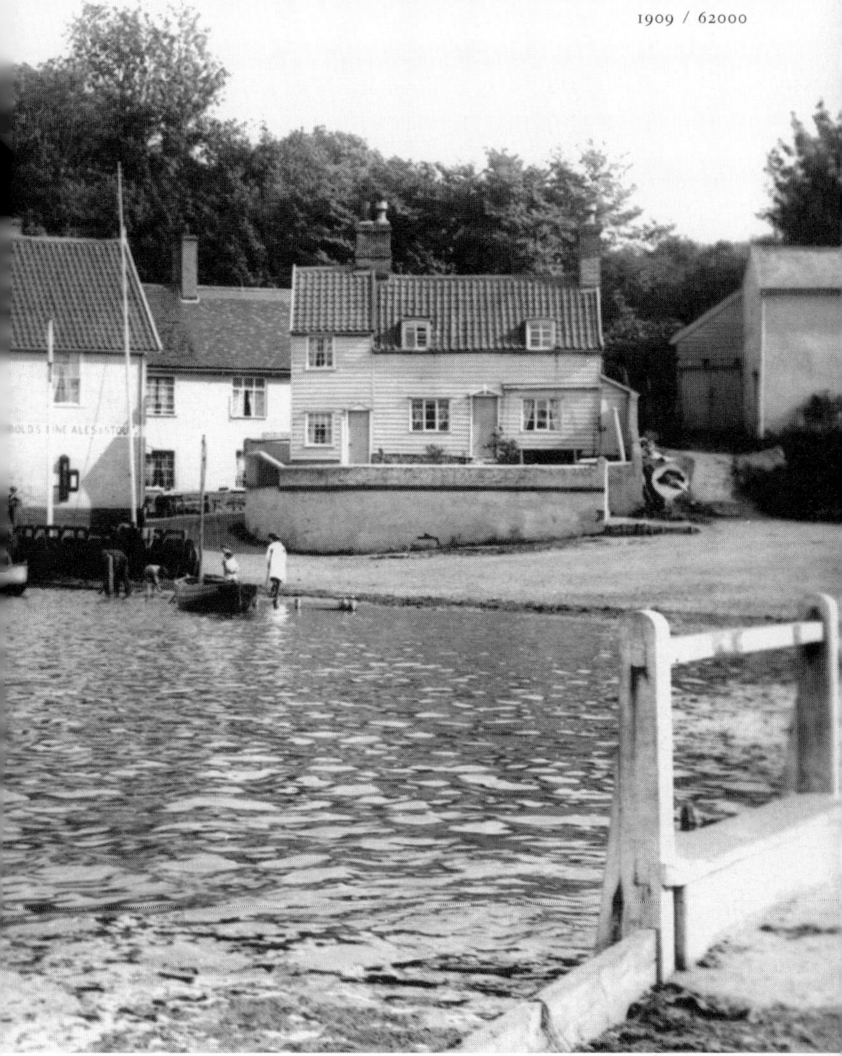

We are looking back from the Butt and Oyster pub towards the boatyard and sailing club. A good deal of boat building and repairing used to go on here, but by now the main industry has gone, and the cottages in the area are more likely to be holiday homes.

PIN MILL
THE BOATYARD

C1960 / P370004

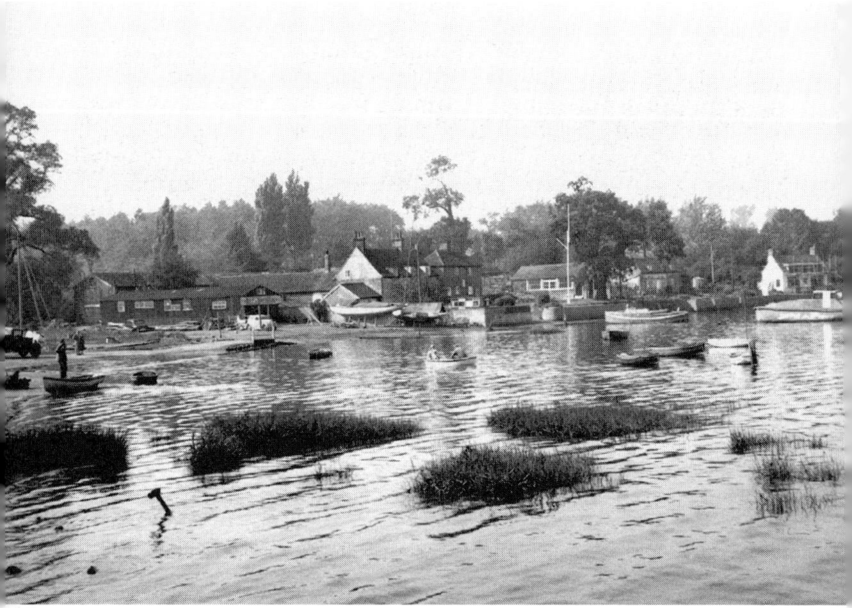

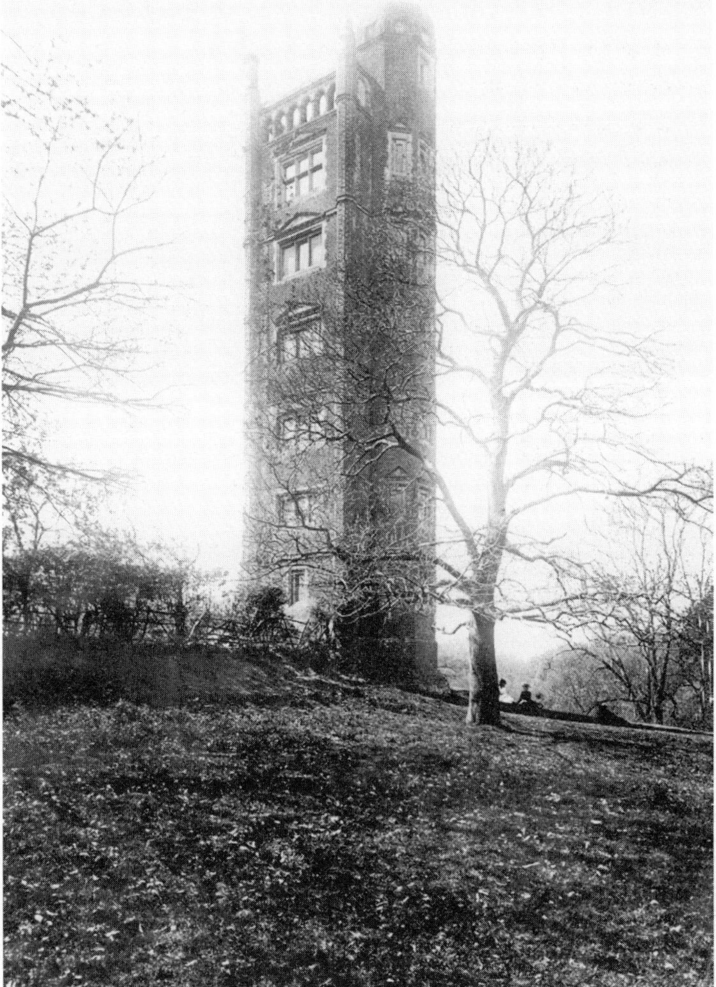

FRESTON TOWER

1893 / 32233

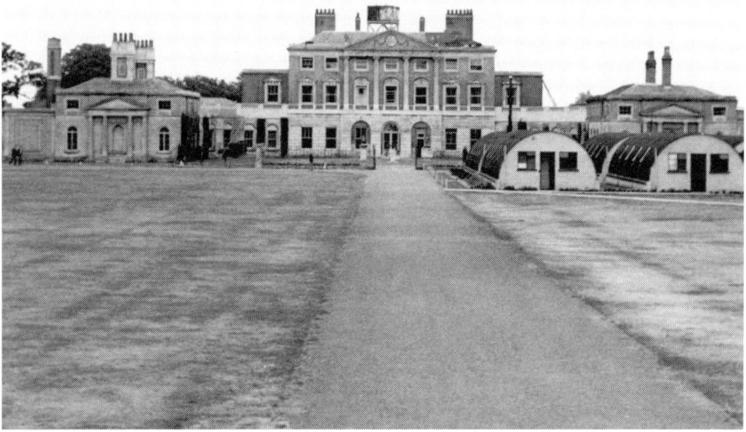

Built in the latter part of the 18th century, Woolverstone Hall was for many years the seat of the Berners family before it was taken over for use as a school.

WOOLVERSTONE HALL

c1960 / W443001

ON THE ORWELL
THE CAT HOUSE

1893 / 32234

Built a hundred years prior to this photograph, this quaint Gothic cottage is named after the white cat painted in the window which overlooks the Orwell. Local legend has it that a stuffed white cat was placed in the window to signal that the coast was clear for smugglers coming ashore.

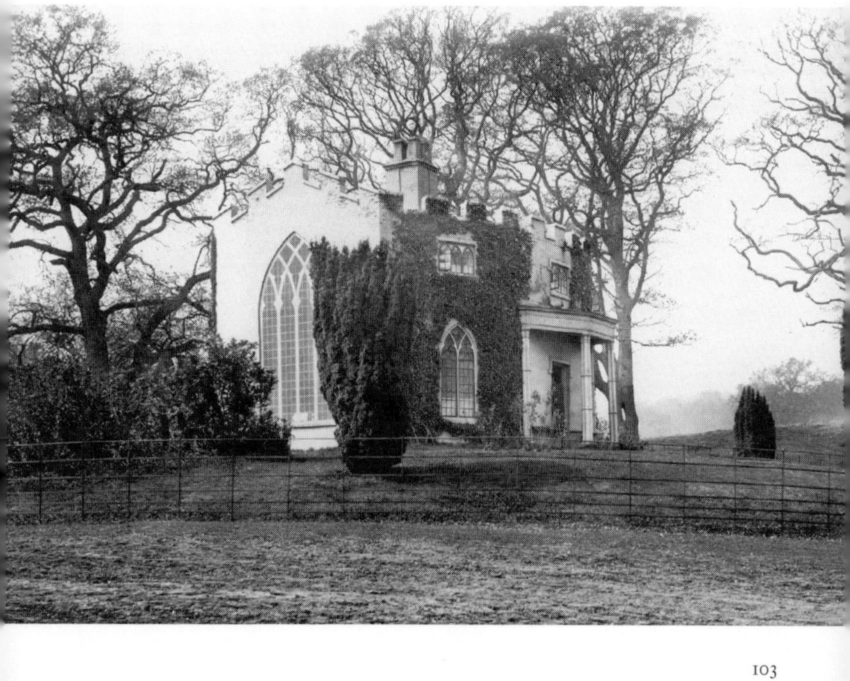

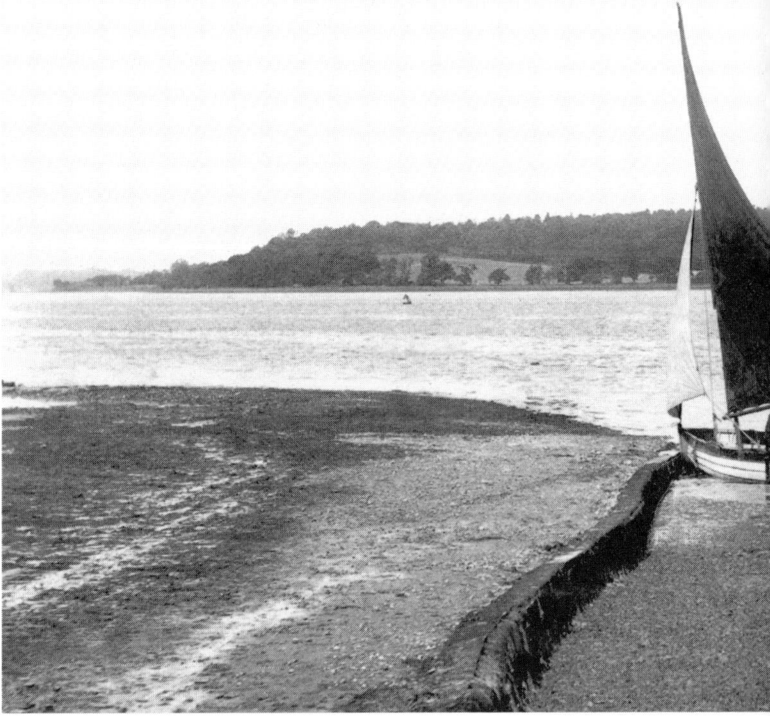

THE RIVER ORWELL FROM FRESTON PARK

1909 / 61997

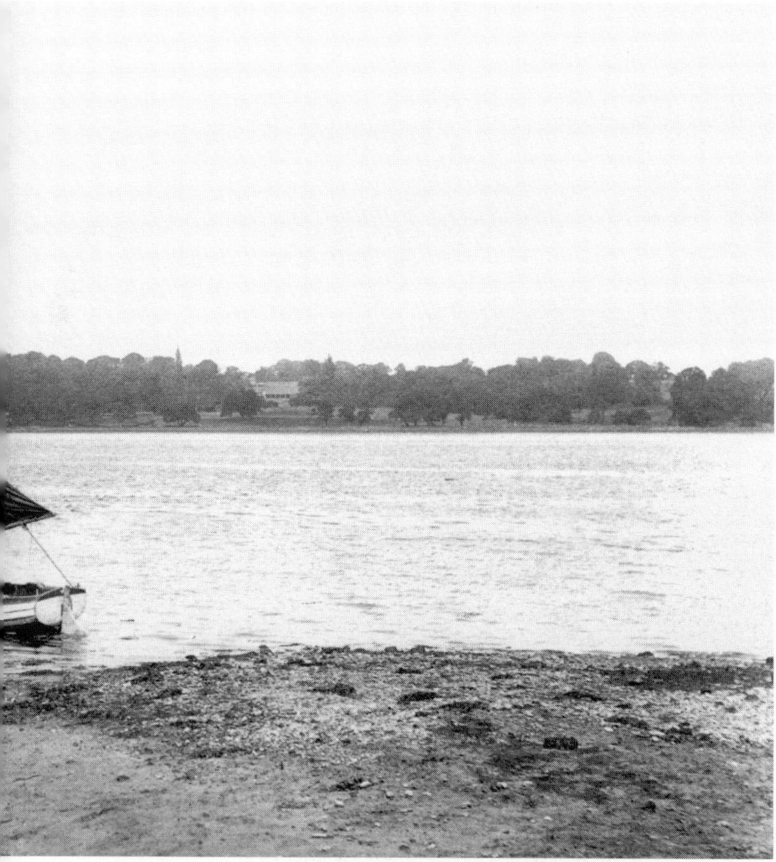

Here we see a sailing boat on the edge of the Orwell below Freston Park. The Royal Harwich Yacht Club is not far away, along with a boatyard and the quaint cottage called the Cat House.

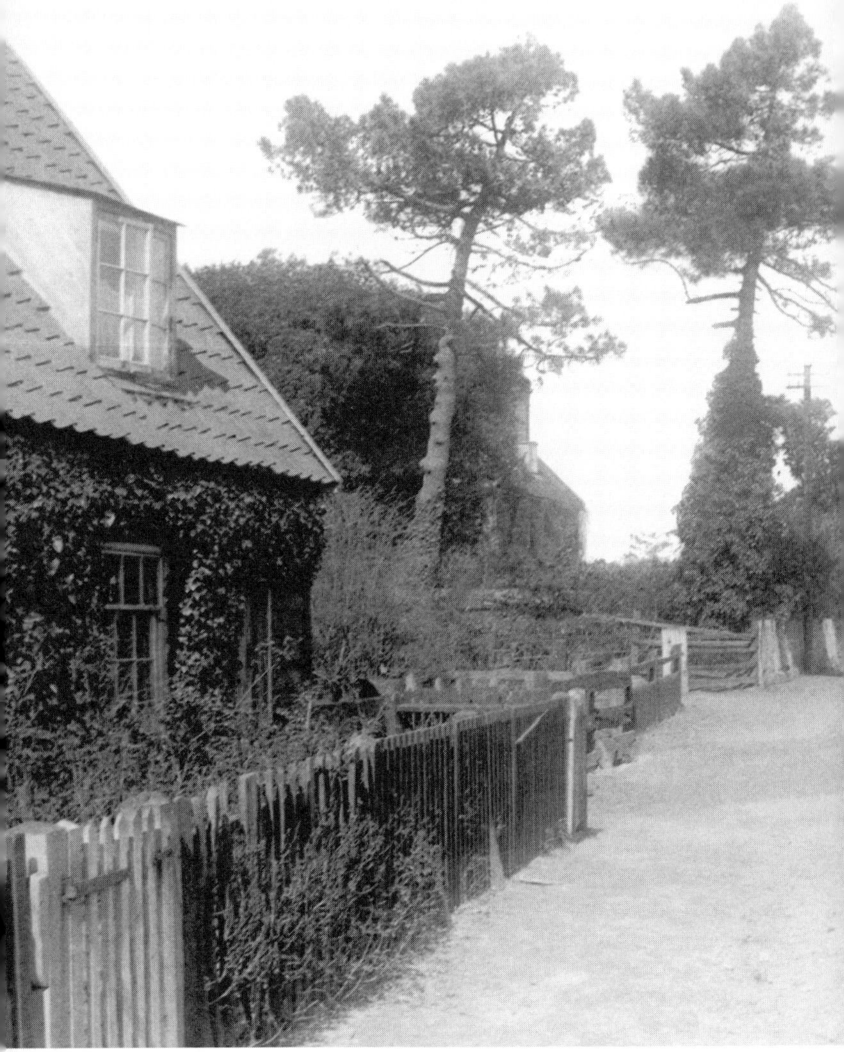

TRIMLEY
THE VILLAGE

1899 / 43250

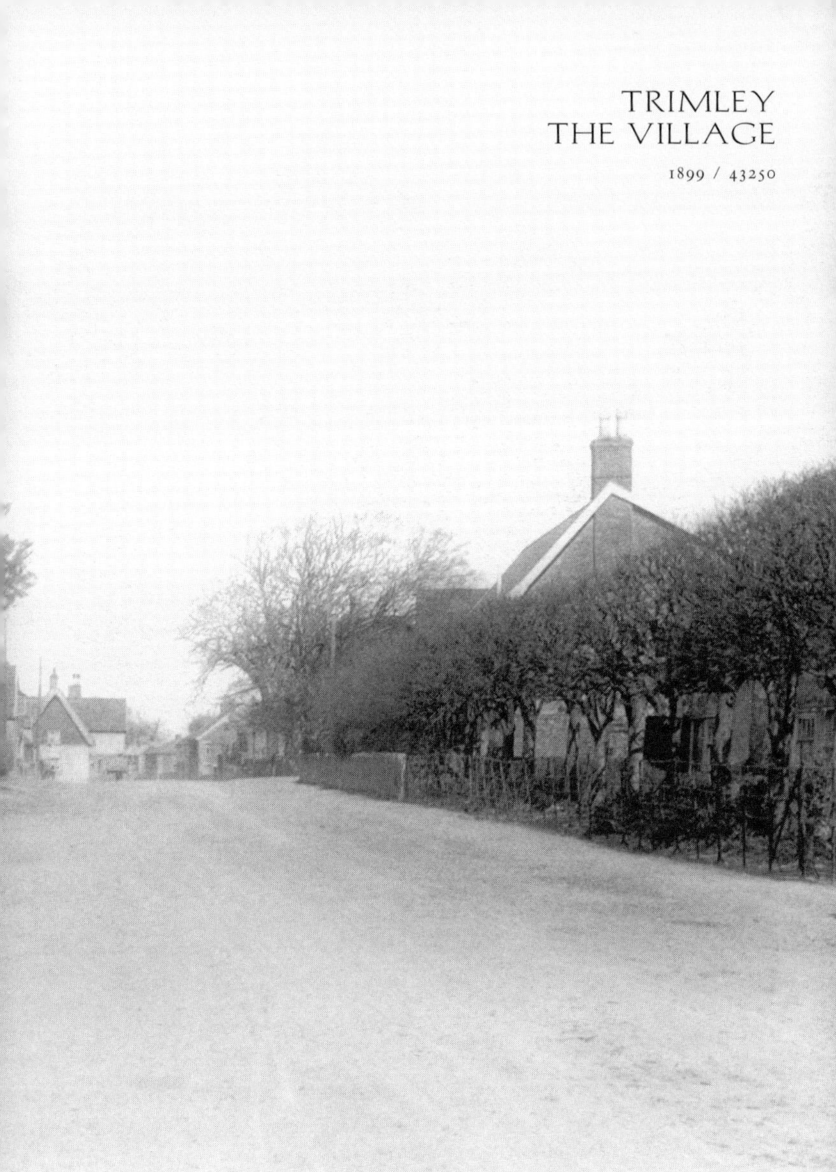

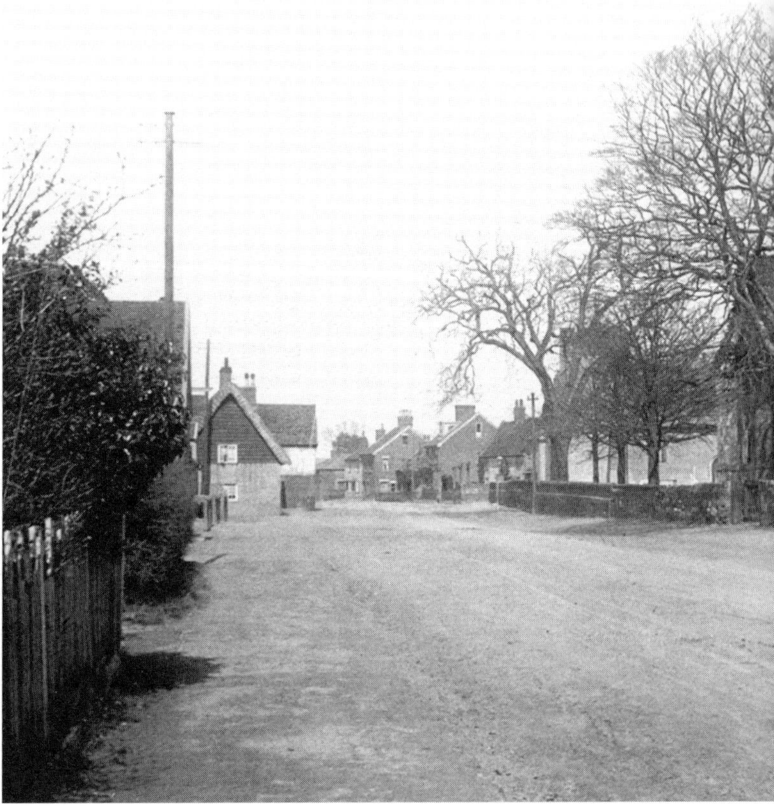

TRIMLEY
THE VILLAGE AND THE CHURCH

1899 / 43248

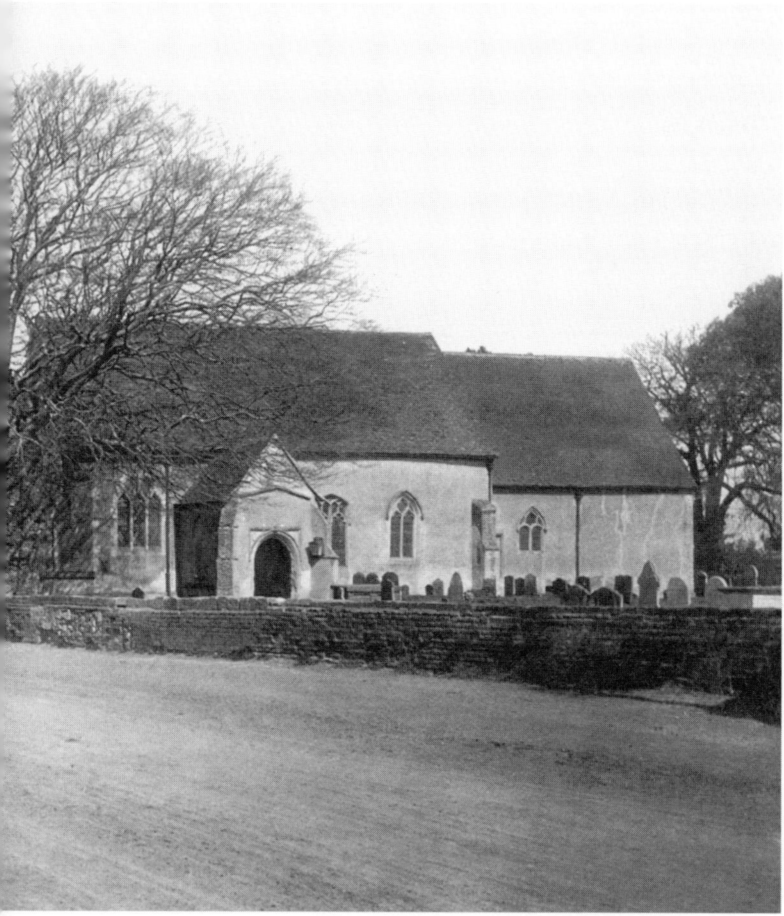

Trimley St Mary and Trimley St Martin lie just outside Felixstowe.

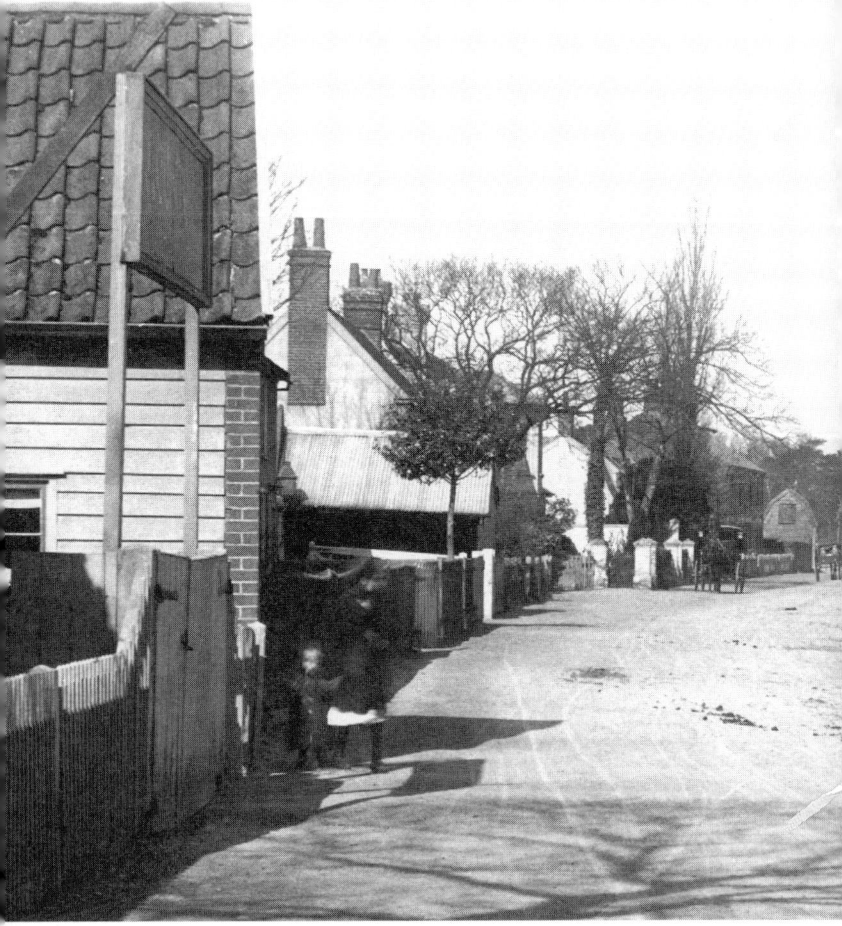

WALTON THE VILLAGE

1899 / 43246

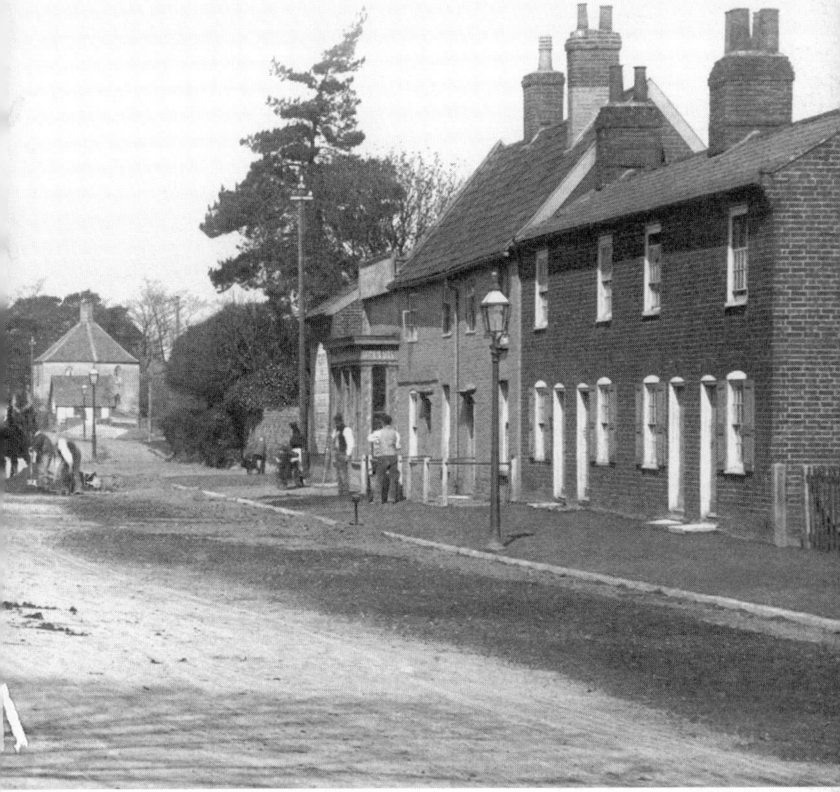

It is a clear and sunny day, but very few people are on the beach. Felixstowe developed as a resort after the Empress of Germany stayed here in 1891.

FELIXSTOWE
THE SEA FRONT

1893 / 32237

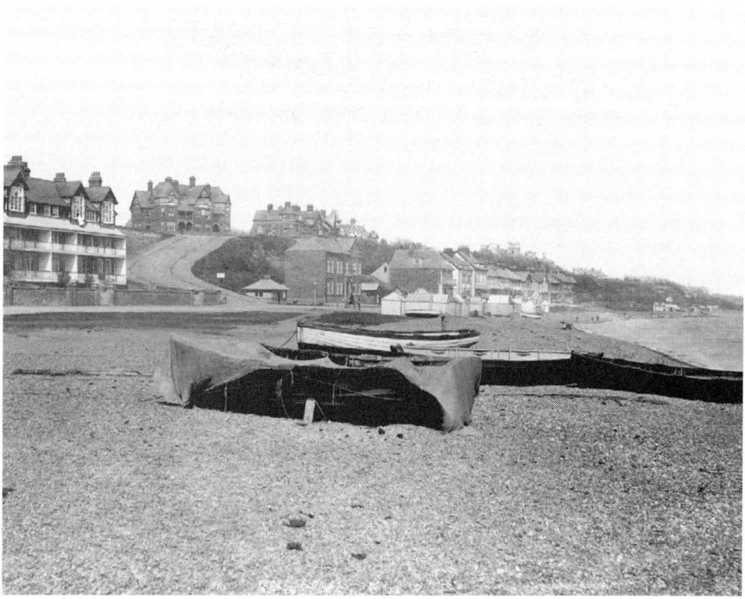

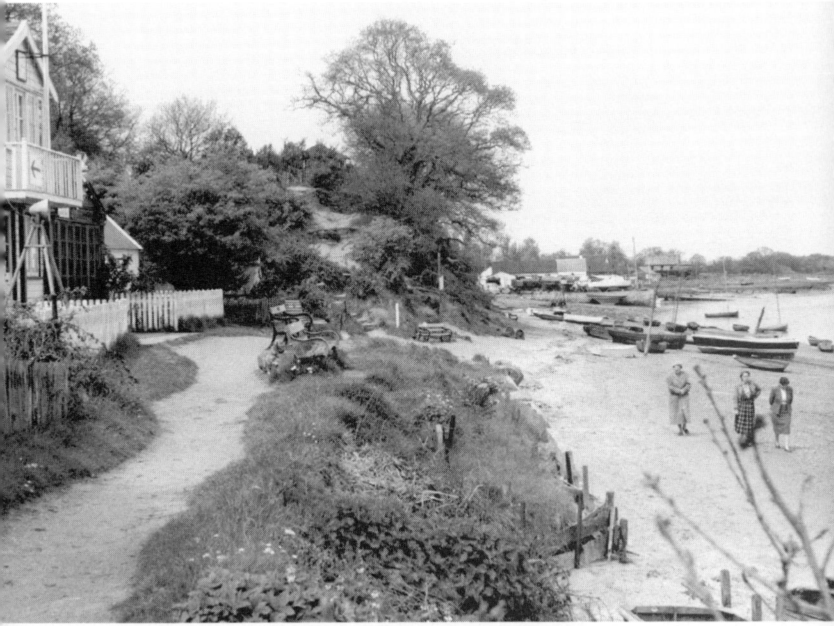

Waldringfield is very much the place for yacht sailors, with its thriving boatyard, yacht club and pub. It is all here because this point along the River Deben has a steep shingle bank upon which boats can be landed or launched at any state of the tide.

WALDRINGFIELD
THE CLUB HOUSE AND THE BEACH

C1960 / W438045

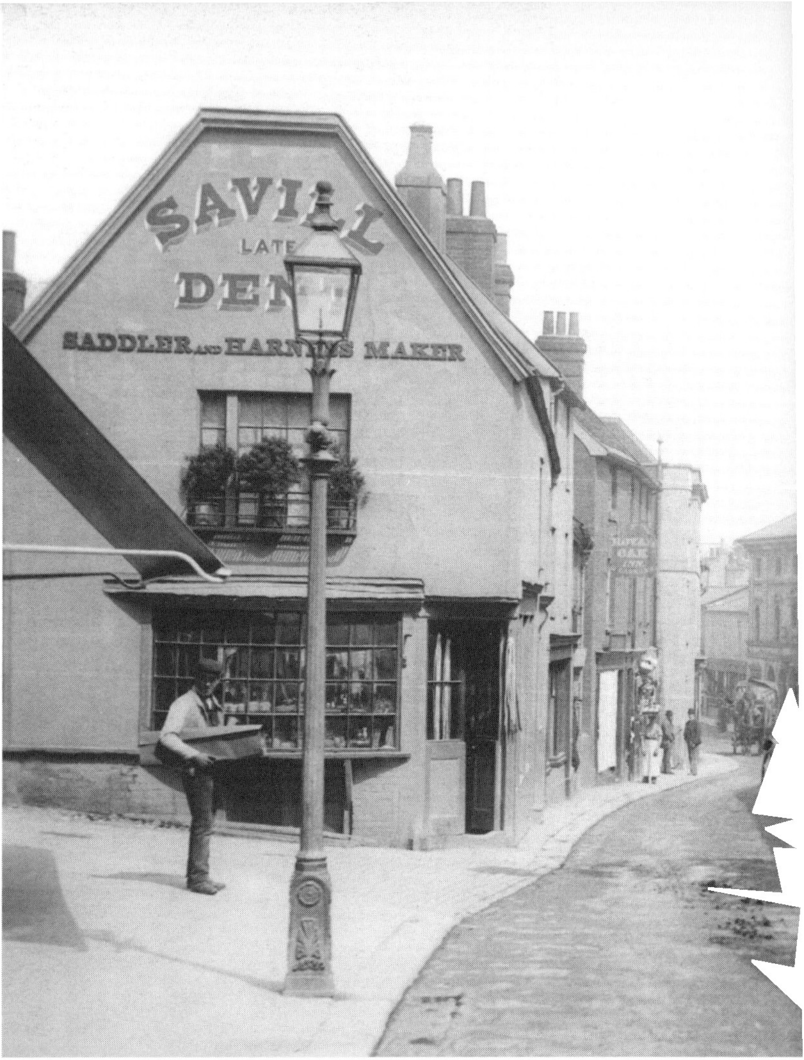

WOODBRIDGE
THE THOROUGHFARE

1894 / 33374

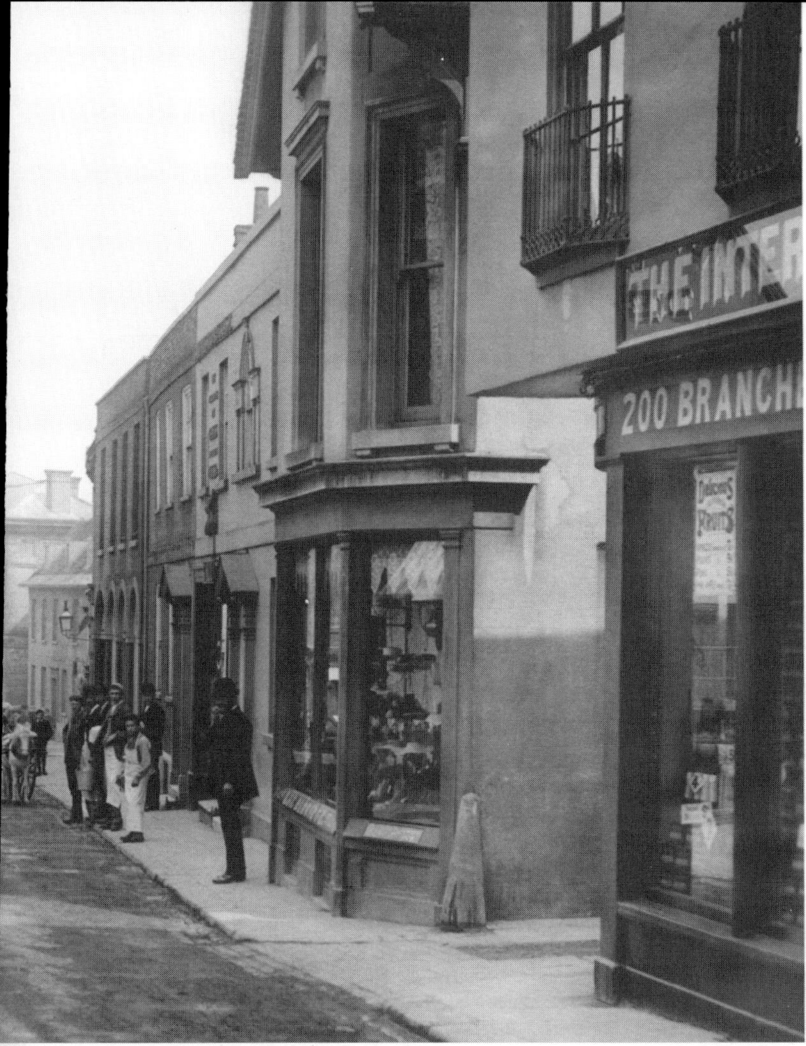

Georgian buildings abound in the town, although it harks back to Tudor times; it owes much of its early development to Thomas Seckford, a lawyer at the court of Elizabeth I.

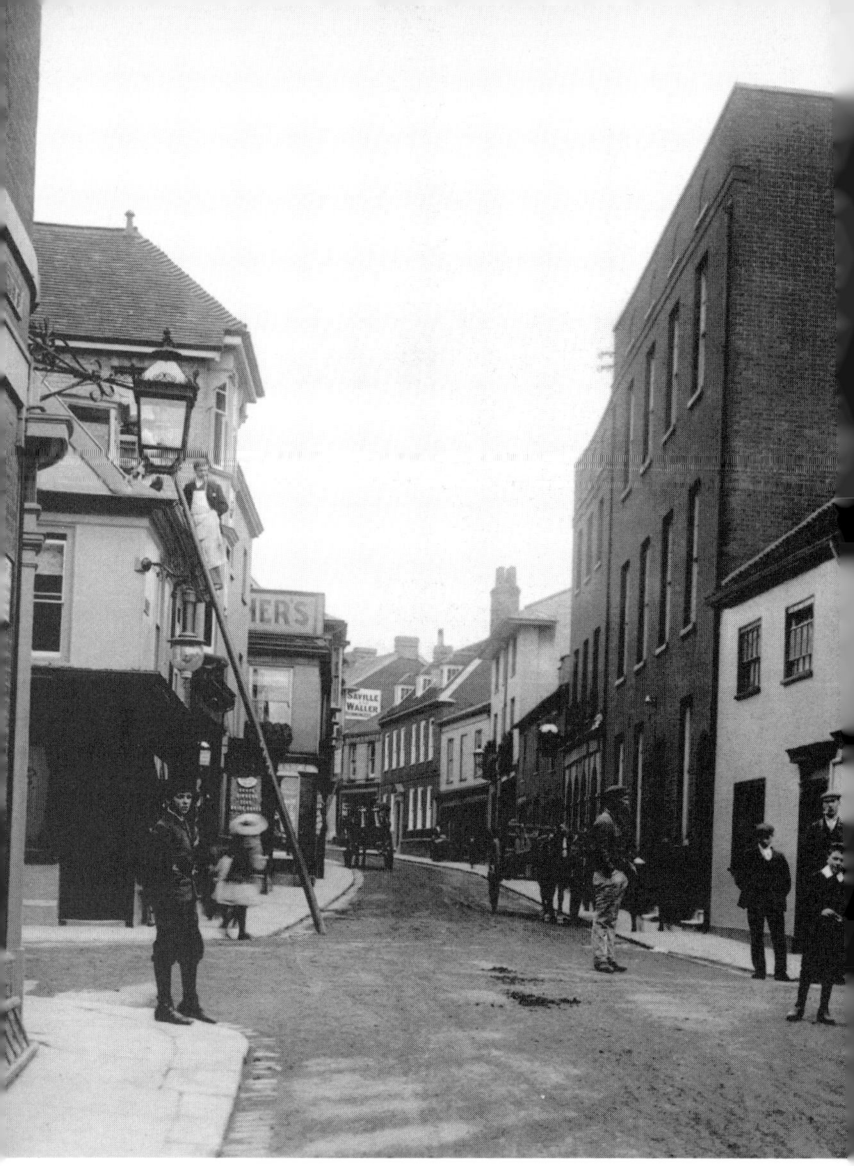
HER'S
SAVILLE
WALLER

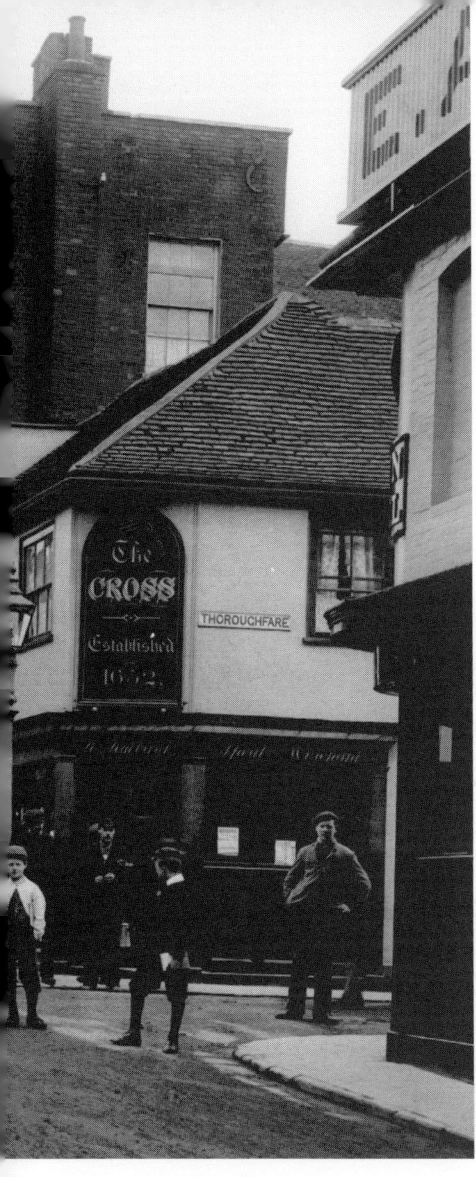

We are looking along Church Street at its junction with Cumberland Street (left) and the Thoroughfare (right). The Cross Public House, which according to its sign was established in 1652, almost certainly took its name from its position on the crossroads.

WOODBRIDGE
CHURCH
STREET

1906 / 53497

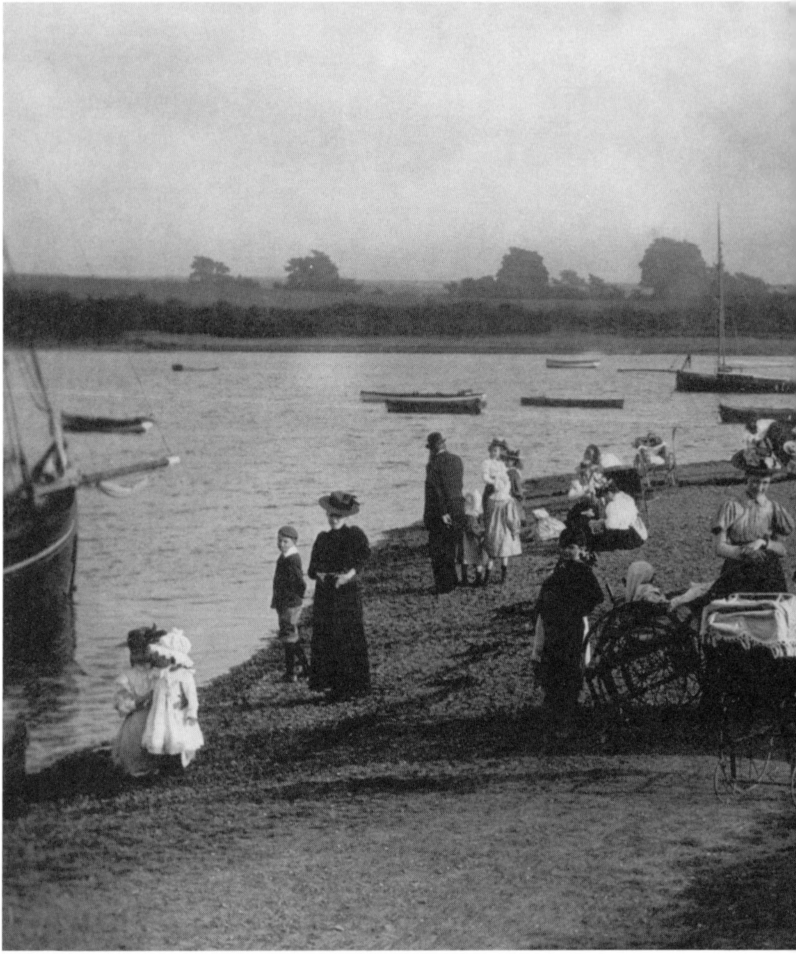

WOODBRIDGE
THE RIVER BANK

1898 / 42772

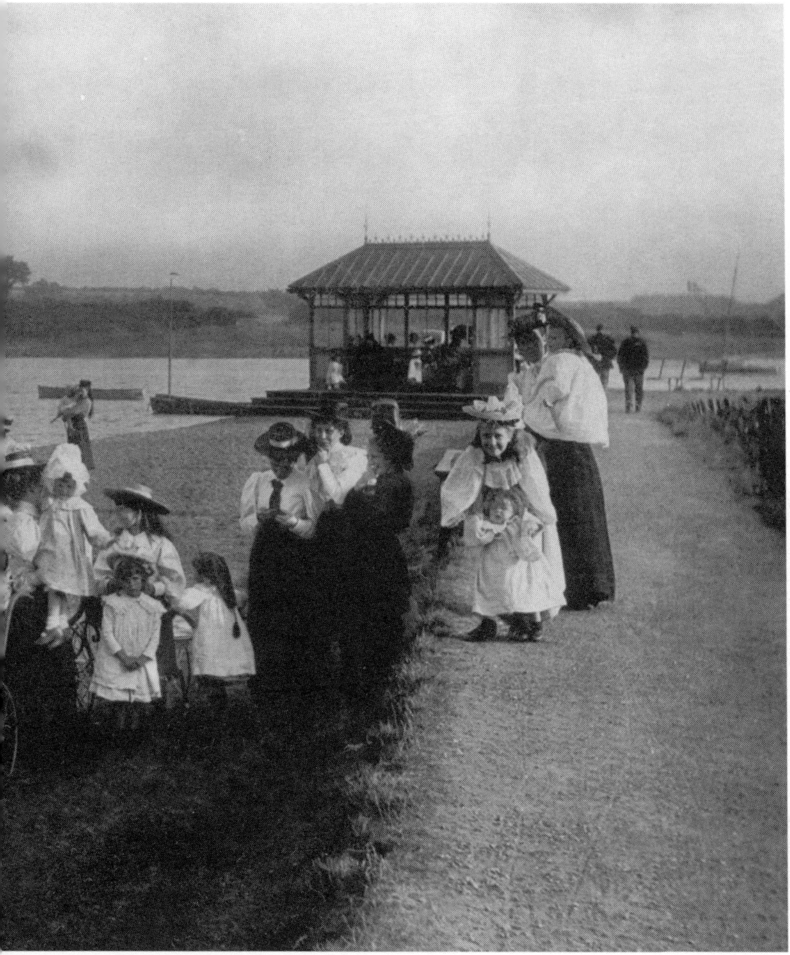

This group of children and their parents or nannies is enjoying the sun and fresh air on the bank of the River Deben.

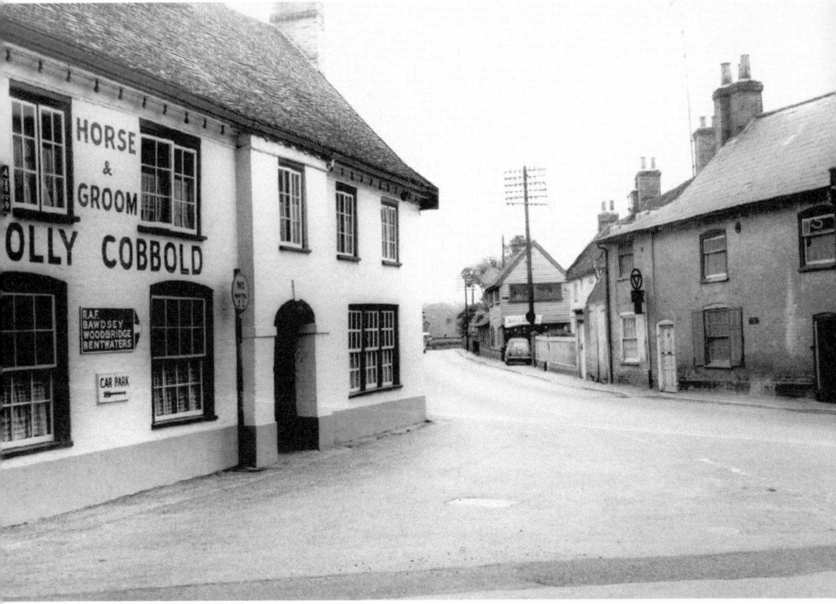

A quiet village on the outskirts of Woodbridge, maybe, but the sign on the pub is a reminder of the concentration of military bases in East Anglia at the height of the Cold War, with the radar station at Bawdsey and two US Air Force bases all within five miles of here.

MELTON
STATION ROAD

C1965 / M268021

Typical 1950s fashions are apparent in this photograph, with long overcoats the norm for a chilly day. The advertising above the shoe shop on the left shows that some favourite products have been around for generations.

MELTON HIGH STREET

C1955 / M268001

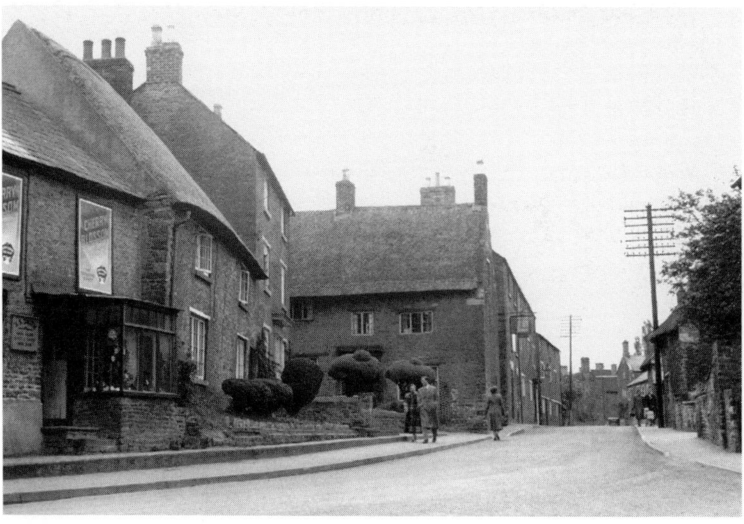

INDEX

PLEASE HELP US BRING FRITH'S PHOTOGRAPHS TO LIFE

Our authors do their best to recount the history of the places they write about. They give insights into how particular towns and villages developed, they describe the architecture of streets and buildings, and they discuss the lives of famous people who lived there. But however knowledgeable our authors are, the story they tell is necessarily incomplete.

Frith's photographs are so much more than plain historical documents. They are living proofs of the flow of human life down the generations. They show real people at real moments in history; and each of those people is the son or daughter of someone, the brother or sister, aunt or uncle, grandfather or grandmother of someone else. All of them lived, worked and played in the streets depicted in Frith's photographs.

We would be grateful if you would tell us about the many places shown in our photographs—the streets with their buildings, shops, businesses and industries. Describe your own memories of life in those streets: what it was like growing up there, who ran the local shop and what shopping was like years ago; if your workplace is shown tell us about your working day and what the building is used for now. With your help more and more Frith photographs can be brought to life, and vital memories preserved for posterity.

We will gradually add your comments and stories to the archive for the benefit of historians of the future. Wherever possible, we will try to include some of your comments in future editions of our books. Moreover, if you spot errors in dates, titles or other facts, please let us know, because our archive records are not always completely accurate—they rely on 150 years of human endeavour and hand-compiled records.

So please write, fax or email us with your stories and memories. Thank you!

FREE PRINT OF YOUR CHOICE

Choose any Frith photograph in this book.
Simply complete the Voucher opposite and return it with your remittance for £2.25 (to cover postage and handling) and we will print the photograph of your choice in SEPIA (size 11 x 8 inches) and supply it in a cream mount with a burgundy rule line
(overall size 14 x 11 inches).
Please note: photographs with a reference number starting with a "Z" are not Frith photographs and cannot be supplied under this offer.
Offer valid for delivery to UK one address only.

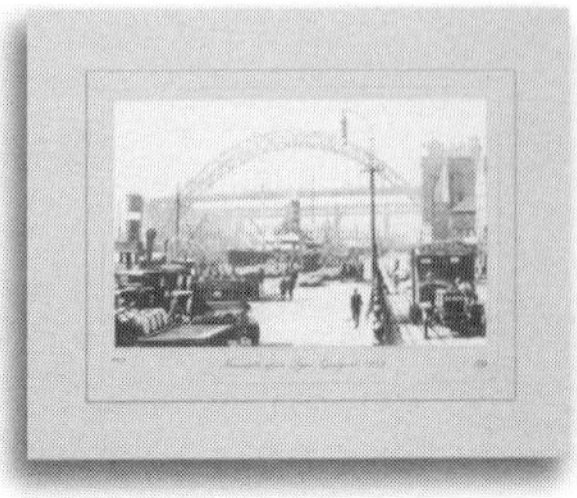

Mounted Print
Overall size 14 x 11 inches (355 x 280mm)

***PLUS:* Order additional Mounted Prints at HALF PRICE - £7.49 each** (normally £14.99)
If you would like to order more Frith prints from this book, possibly as gifts for friends and family, you can buy them at half price (with no additional postage and handling costs).

***PLUS:* Have your Mounted Prints framed**
For an extra £14.95 per print you can have your mounted print(s) framed in an elegant polished wood and gilt moulding, overall size 16 x 13 inches (no additional postage and handling required).

IMPORTANT!

These special prices are only available if you use this form to order. You must use the ORIGINAL VOUCHER (no copies permitted).

We can only despatch to one UK address. This offer cannot be combined with any other offer.

FRITH PRODUCTS AND SERVICES

All Frith photographs are available for you to buy as framed or mounted prints. From time to time, other illustrated items such as Address Books and Maps are also available. Already, almost 80,000 Frith archive photographs can be viewed and purchased on the internet through the Frith website.

For more detailed information on Frith companies and products, visit:

www.francisfrith.co.uk

For further information, or trade enquiries, contact:

The Francis Frith Collection, Frith's Barn, Teffont, Salisbury SP3 5QP
Tel: +44 (0) 1722 716 376 Fax: +44 (0) 1722 716 881 Email: sales@francisfrith.co.uk

Voucher

for FREE and Reduced Price Frith Prints

Do not photocopy this voucher. Only the original is valid, so please fill it in, cut it out and return it to us with your order.

	Picture ref no	Page number	Qty	Mounted @ £7.49	Framed + £14.95	Orders Total £
1			1	**Free of charge***	£	£
2				£7.49	£	£
3				£7.49	£	£
4				£7.49	£	£
5				£7.49	£	£
6				£7.49	£	£
				* Post & handling		£3.50
				Total Order Cost		£

Please allow 28 days for delivery. Offer available to one UK address only

Title of this book . . . .

I enclose a cheque / postal order for £ . . . .
payable to 'The Francis Frith Collection'

OR debit my Mastercard / Visa / Maestro / Amex card

Card Number

Issue No (Maestro only) Valid from (Amex/Maestro)

Expires Signature

Name Mr/Mrs/Ms ....

Address ....

....

....

..............................Postcode..............................

Daytime Tel No ....

E-mail ....

Valid to 31/12/07

Send completed Voucher form to:

The Francis Frith Collection, Frith's Barn, Teffont, Salisbury, Wiltshire SP3 5QP England

If you need more space, please write your address on a separate sheet of paper.